Personal Equity Plans

A **Daily Telegraph**
Investor's Handbook

Personal Equity Plans

Richard Northedge

Published by Telegraph Publications,
Peterborough Court, At South Quay,
181 Marsh Wall, London E14 9SR

Series Editor: Marlene Garsia

Typeset by Quadraset Ltd, Avon
Printed by Biddles Ltd, Guildford

ISBN 0 86367 229 9

A pep talk from Abbey National.

Consider for a moment the attractions of a PEP with Abbey National.

One of Britain's largest building societies, we have a proven track record of earning power and security.

With our PEP, we always maintain Unit Trust holdings at the permitted maximum with the rest in shares, thus spreading the risk whilst maintaining a high growth potential.

In addition, we draw upon the investment expertise of Fidelity, one of the world's largest investment management groups.

What is more, just £420, or £35 a month, will open a plan.

Abbey National has a national network of branches, each one dedicated to maintaining the high levels of service that over eight million people rely on. So you'll always find us very easy to approach.

For an information pack and application form, ring 0800 414161 or contact your local branch.

FIDELITY NOMINEES LTD.,
RIVER WALK, TONBRIDGE, KENT.

ABBEY NATIONAL BUILDING SOCIETY,
ABBEY HOUSE, BAKER STREET, LONDON NW1 6XL.

Contents

INTRODUCTION

'Investment in personal equity plans has been carefully designed to be as simple as possible for the first-time shareholder' – Chancellor of the Exchequer, Nigel Lawson.

There are many different types of investment. Some we think of as such and make calculated decisions when selecting them and deciding whether to commit our funds; some we have we may not actually consider as investments. A bank or building society account, for instance, earning interest, fits into the investment category, but to the account holder may merely be a convenient place to put money between receiving it and spending it.

A house is an investment, and has been a good one to those people who have seen their property's value rise by 10 per cent or even 25 per cent each year – though it was most likely bought as a place to live rather than as a vehicle for accumulating wealth, and considerations such as proximity to schools, the size of the garden or the type of heating probably figured more in the selection of the property than the prospects of it rising in value. The endowment policy which is probably being used to repay the loan that enabled the house to be bought is also an investment – though to most people the endowment policy was probably taken out as a protection against one of the householders suffering an accident or because it tax-efficiently brought down the monthly cost of the mortgage.

Few people concern themselves that the premiums on the endowment policy are used by the life assurance company to invest in the stock market – not only in Britain, but in New York or Tokyo or on the Continent. It is only the profits of those international shares which allow house-buyers to own their own homes outright; ultimately, however, few of them realise it.

Similarly, the regular pension fund contributions which employers make on their staff's behalf, or which workers themselves make, are invested in a variety of ways from government stocks to city-centre office blocks, but mainly in shares of the big companies of Britain and abroad.

People who wonder whether they should start investing in the stock market may find that they have already started without knowing it. Though having never dealt with a stockbroker, he or she may already be a substantial investor in shares through a pension fund or life assurance policy. Knowing that may make them less worried about moving further into the world of share ownership.

It is, of course, possible to own shares directly in some of the largest companies in the country and still never to have used the services of a stockbroker or other share-dealing agent. The privatisation programme by the government of recent years has enabled the public to buy shares in British Telecom, British Gas, Rolls-Royce, British Airways, Jaguar, BAA, British Aerospace and British Petroleum – all with no more bother than filling in the coupon in a newspaper as though they were purchasing mail-order goods (even if few chose to buy BP).

Add in TSB Group and a range of other shares in private companies which have been floated on the London stock market in similar, if usually less publicised ways, and the so-called small investor could have a portfolio of shares in a wide section of British business, from Andrew Lloyd Webber's Really Useful Group through specialist retailers such as Tie Rack or Sock Shop to the blue-blooded City bank, Morgan Grenfell. The investor may never have thought of using a word as grand as 'portfolio' for the collection of certificates that has accumulated, each often representing an original investment of just £250 or less but now actually worth considerably more than that.

Direct share ownership in Britain has more than trebled

since 1979 to the point where 8.5 million people owned a share in one company or another at the start of 1987. The offers of shares in British Airways, BAA, Rolls-Royce and BP will only have increased that. The figure represented one adult in every five, and means, for instance, that with the latest share offers, there are more share owners than there are mortgage-holders and more than there are trade union members. Times have changed considerably, though the population still possibly remains a nation of share applicants rather than share buyers. More than three-quarters of those share owners held investments in nothing more than TSB or the privatisations whose well-promoted coupons appeared in the press – it is a far smaller proportion of the population who are now in the habit of telephoning their stockbroker and asking to buy shares in one of the many companies whose shares have not been sold with the ease and razzamatazz of the privatisations, even such good names as J Sainsbury or ICI.

The steady rise in the prices of shares quoted on the London stock market since 1979 has done nothing to dis-courage people from becoming share investors for the first time, or to add to their existing holdings, of course. Until the great crash of October 1987, Stock Exchange profits had looked easy. While there had been a number of hiccups over the years, which had caused share prices to fall sufficiently on one day for the decline to warrant alarming headlines on the evening's television news or morning papers, there were less publicised gains shortly afterward which more than made up the losses. The *Financial Times'* Ordinary Share Index, a direct measure of 30 leading shares, started with a value of 100 in 1935. It was 20 years before the index briefly touched 200; it reached 300 in 1960, 400 in 1967, and 500 in 1968, whereupon markets fell back below 350 before recovering to 500 in 1972. In 1974 the three-day week, secondary banking crashes and the oil crisis knocked the index back to below 150. But from then until October 1987 share prices did not look back. The FT index was back up to 300 in early 1975, 400 the following year, through 500 in 1977, onto 1,000 in 1985 then 1,100 and 1,200 the same year, 1,300 and 1,400 in 1986 and then in 1987 alone the index soared through 1,500 to more than 1,900 before the crash knocked it back below 1,250.

Even with the crash, anyone who had held shares for a couple of years was still probably showing a profit – and they would also have been receiving dividends from most of their shares once or twice a year.

The growth in share prices has been spectacular, though this book will emphasise later that there are dangers in such investment and at least the 1987 crash reminded people that there is a risk, despite the preceding year's steady rise in prices. The rise was nevertheless a useful background for the government not only to sell shares in nationalised companies against, but also to support one of its political objectives, turning Britain into a nation of share owners.

Not all those who have bought shares for the first time in recent years are supporters of a Conservative government or its ideologies, of course, any more than all bank customers would declare themselves supporters of a capitalist system, but Mrs Thatcher and her Chancellor, Nigel Lawson, have committed themselves to turning the country into one where people are keen to take a serious interest in their investments. Previous governments have already converted the country into a nation of home owners: the six million or more people who have bought shares for the first time since 1979 suggest that the objective has already been met to a substantial extent. Indeed, already Mrs Thatcher and Mr Lawson have embarked on their next task, attempting to make us show the same interest in our pension schemes as we do in our houses and increasingly in shares.

The trend towards home ownership has been helped not only by the dearth of rented accommodation and the tendency for prices to rise plus the ready source of mortgage finance, but also by tax concessions. The interest paid on up to £30,000 of that mortgage can be offset against income, so reducing the monthly costs significantly – no such concession applies to borrowing for other purposes. The endowment policies which the majority of the population use for repaying their mortgages allows that income tax relief to be maximised, but a tax concession also means that the income earned on the stocks and shares that the policy buys is tax-free too, and the investments can be sold with no tax on the profit.

Indeed, on policies issued before the 1984 budget there was, and remains, a tax relief on the premiums paid on those policies, which effectively cut their cost by over 17 per cent. And when the house or flat is sold, there is no capital gains tax to pay on the profit above the original cost as there is on other investments. No wonder we have become a nation of home owners; we have been given a considerable financial encouragement to be so, and the government still operates a Homeloan scheme giving modest free cash and loans to first-time buyers.

Similar tax concessions exist to encourage us to become more involved in our pensions too. Up to quite generous limits, the contributions from our pay are deducted without the subtraction of income tax. Once in the pension fund there is again no tax on the income from the investments bought and no tax on their sale and a large part of the pension investment can ultimately be taken out of the fund in a lump-sum without the payment of any tax. Britons have traditionally glazed over at the mention of pensions, but governments have given some very attractive financial reasons why we should show interest.

Shares remained a Cinderella, however. There is a tax to pay when they are bought, though this stamp duty does not apply to the new shares bought through privatisations and other flotations. Income tax is payable in full on dividends received, and is deducted at the basic rate before the company even sends out its cheque. Any shareholders who do not pay income tax have to go to the trouble of recovering the tax already deducted – high-rate taxpayers still have to pay the extra. And when the shares are sold the investor has a liability to capital gains tax on his profit. It was in his 1986 budget, therefore, that Nigel Lawson resolved to add share owning to the list of investments which would have tax incentives to encourage us to participate. He declared that from 1987 it would be possible to invest in shares through a new product to be called a Personal Equity Plan.

1 WHAT ARE PEPS?

On March 18, 1986 the House of Commons was packed for the Chancellor of the Exchequer's budget speech. Nigel Lawson had told his cabinet colleagues that morning what this, his third such speech, was to contain: other MPs and radio listeners had to wait.

Mr Lawson took his audience through the usual analysis of the state of the economy and its world context – the fall in oil prices, an increase in Britain's net overseas assets, target ranges for the MO and £M3 monetary indicators, through public sector borrowing requirements and tax allowances on mines and oil wells. There was little here to interest the ordinary man waiting to hear how much petrol or beer or cigarettes would have to rise in price. Then came the Chancellor's surprise.

'Just as we have made Britain a nation of home owners, it is the long-term ambition of this government to make the British people a nation of share owners too; to create a popular capitalism in which more and more men and women have a direct personal stake in British business and industry. Both through the rapid growth of employee share schemes and through the outstandingly successful privatisation programme, much progress has been made.

'But not enough. Nor I fear will we ever achieve our goal so long as the tax system continues to discriminate so heavily in favour of institutional investment rather than direct share ownership.

'Accordingly, I propose to introduce a radical new scheme to encourage direct investment in UK equities. Starting next January, any adult will be able to invest up to £200 a month

15

or £2,400 a year in shares. These will be held in a special account which I am calling a Personal Equity Plan. So long as the investment is kept in the plan for a relatively short minimum period of between one and two years, all re-invested dividends and all capital gains on disposals will be entirely free of tax. The longer the investment is kept in the plan, the more the tax relief will build up and the greater will be the benefits. And there will normally be no need for the Inland Revenue to get involved at all.

'Although the scheme is designed for everyone, it is specially designed to encourage smaller savers and particularly those who may never previously have invested in equities in their lives. So the plans will be simple and flexible to operate. Anyone who is legally able to deal in securities will be eligible to register as a plan manager, but the investor himself will own the shares, and the rights that go with them, including voting rights. And it will be for the investor to choose whether to make the investment decisions himself, or to give the plan manager authority to act on his behalf.

'The cost of the scheme will be about £25 million in 1987–88 but will build up in later years as more plans are taken out. This is a substantial, innovative and exciting new scheme. I am confident that over time, it will bring about a dramatic extension of share ownership in Britain. Although wholly different in structure from the *Loi Monory* in France, I expect it to be every bit as successful in achieving its objective. I am sure that this whole house will welcome this far-reaching package of measures to reform the taxation of savings and investments.

'I now turn to the tax treatment of charities', continued the Chancellor, but already the commentators and those involved in the investment industry were thinking back over what Mr Lawson had promised. Ordinary investors were to be allowed to buy shares and receive their dividends and capital profits without paying any tax, just as the investment managers of pension funds do. This was a tax-break for the small investor that had not been expected: added to a budget announcement of the halving to 0.5 per cent in the stamp duty paid when shares are bought anyway, it gave share-ownership the tax incentive that previously applied only to housing or pensions.

The 'equities' of Mr Lawson's personal equity plans are merely another word for shares, as are 'securities'. The *Loi Monory* which he mentioned is a French law which allows private investors to offset the cost of their shares against their income tax, rather like pension fund contributions in Britain, or mortgage interest. Initially, at least, personal equity plans are less generous than the French incentive, but it was better than anything which had been available to British share buyers for 25 years.

Before that Budget night was out, the personal equity plans had been dubbed with the acronym PEPs, but investors still had to wait until 1987 before they could commit their money, and that gave several months to consider whether PEPs really were going to be a bargain after all.

Details of the plans emerged in the year's Finance Bill and through a series of ministerial announcements. Details changed too as the government gave in to pleas from various parties who would be involved in devising and marketing PEPs. But the final version proved not very different from what Mr Lawson had announced to the House of Commons.

Up to £200 a month or £2,400 a year can be invested in a PEP
It is for individual companies offering PEPs to decide what minimum investment they will accept: some will take £20 a month, some £420 a year. A few PEP managers will accept only the maximum £2,400 in one annual payment.

Only one PEP can be invested in during any calendar year
It is illegal for one person to invest in two PEPs during the same year – even if, say, only £1,000 was put in each, keeping the total investment within the £2,400 maximum. It would be possible to put £2,400 into a PEP at the end of December 1988 and £2,400 into the same company's PEP or a different one a few days later in January 1989 because they are different calendar years.

Some PEP money can remain in cash and the interest is tax-free too

There are rules about how much of the investor's money can be in cash and how it has to be held, but the interest earned will be entirely free of income tax so long as it is added into the existing PEP money. Given that both banks and building societies must by law deduct tax before paying interest (only the government's National Savings need not) this is a valuable concession.

Interest of 10 per cent is worth only 7.3 per cent after deducting basic-rate income tax: higher rate taxpayers would see that cut further, with 60 per cent taxpayers receiving only 4 per cent net. Put another way, a top-rate taxpayer would have to find an investment paying 25 per cent elsewhere to be left with the same 10 per cent obtainable inside a personal equity plan.

The amount of cash that can be left inside a PEP at any one time is discussed later, but for the first year the whole £2,400 can remain liquid instead of being used to buy shares.

Dividends on the shares bought through the PEP are tax-free

Most companies pay out part of their profits or past profits as a dividend to shareholders. Most big companies actually make two payments a year. In some way these payments are comparable to the interest received from an investment in a bank or building society account, but there are differences and they can fluctuate even more than interest rates, particularly at companies with erratic profit performances.

An ordinary shareholder not investing through a PEP would find that the dividend payments came with basic-rate income tax already deducted. The shareholder is even slightly worse off than the bank account holder whose interest is received with tax deducted, because while the dividend is reduced by the whole basic tax rate – 27 per cent in 1987–88 – banks and building societies need subtract only 24¾ per cent, which is a special tax rate to average out their taxpaying customers with those who would not normally have had to pay income tax. Like the bank depositors, shareholders whose total income makes them higher-rate taxpayers have to pay the extra above the standard rate, but unlike depositors, shareholders whose income is too low to make them income tax payers can claim back the tax wrongly deducted on their dividends.

PEPs investors, however, face no tax on their dividends even though their incomes put them inside the tax-paying brackets, and they do not suffer the problems of having to claim back small amounts of tax from the Inland Revenue because PEP managers will do that for them.

Profits when PEP investments are sold are tax-free
Normally, when shareholders sell their investments at a profit they become liable to capital gains tax. Since 1965 this tax has been levied at a flat 30 per cent (there are no higher rate bands as there are with income tax or inheritance tax, for instance). The tax applies to most realised investment gains with the notable exceptions of government gilt-edged stock and anyone's main house (though it is payable on second homes that are sold).

Just as a certain amount of income can be earned by anyone in a particular year before income tax has to be paid, a certain amount can be realised before capital gains tax is due. For the 1987–88 tax year this is £6,600, and if that exemption rises in line with inflation as is usual, it will be about £6,900 in 1988–89.

It is because most small investors with only a few hundred pounds invested in British Telecom or Rolls-Royce are not making such large profits in a year, or are still holding their shares and have not yet realised their profits (if indeed they realise that they have made such profits on paper), that many small investors have been untroubled by capital gains tax. Even small investors selling small quantities of shares whose value, never mind profit, is below £6,600 must declare the sales on tax forms, however.

If the tax was a straight 30 per cent of all the gains as they are taken, it would be a simple deduction, if an annoying one. Unfortunately it is the complexity of the calculations which make capital gains tax the most hated tax in Britain, not the amount of the principal or gains being taxed. There are more complicated taxes, but they affect only very few people or companies and usually only for large sums of money which justify paying for professional help from accountants or others.

Even ignoring any financial advantages, relieving PEPs investors of the problem of calculating a capital gains tax liability gives personal equity plans a considerable advantage. Remember those words of Mr Lawson to the House of Commons: 'There will normally be no need for the Inland Revenue to get involved at all.'

And because the taxman need not be told of a person's PEP, neither need a spouse or any other relative. Women who resent having to divulge their financial affairs to their husbands for him to put on his tax form, as is usually necessary in Britain, can thus invest in a PEP and keep the matter secret, or at least feel that they have an investment in their own right which does not have to be grouped with a husband's. Other dependent relatives can similarly preserve their privacy.

Because there is no capital gains tax, investors can ignore it and ignore the rest of this section. But lest anyone doubt what an advantage it is to be allowed to ignore the tax, they may wish to read a highly simplified version of the tax calculations they are avoiding.

A capital gain is the difference between the price paid for an investment and the price at which it is sold. Let's say 1,000 shares were bought for 97½p each, making £975, and sold for 197½p, or £1,975. That would be a £1,000 gain – except that the investor is allowed to add his buying costs, say £25, to the shares' cost and to subtract the selling costs, say £50. The gain would be £1,925 minus £1,000 therefore, making £925 – except that the investor can also allow for inflation. If the official retail prices index had risen 20 per cent between the purchase and the sale, then the £1,000 adjusted purchase price is really worth £1,200 at the time the shares were sold, so the gain on the £1,925 adjusted sale proceeds is only £725. That £725 is clearly inside the annual exemption limit, but the investor has to make similar calculations for all the other investments he has sold – not only shares, but unit trusts or property too. In each case it is necessary to find the rise in the retail prices index between the relevant buying and selling dates (except that for investments before March 1982 there are special rules) and any losses realised can also be deducted.

But, as we stated, that was a simple example. Imagine 500 of the shares had been bought for 90p and the other 500 for 105p giving the same £975 total. What if only 500 were sold later at 197½p: even before the dealing cost and inflation adjustments, what is the profit per share – 107½p or 92½p? Or should the small investor try averaging his buying prices? Imagine the company had made an offer of new shares at 75p which the investor had taken up, or that it had given away free bonus shares as companies often do; how then is the calculation made? There is a correct answer to each of the questions of course, but finding them requires an expert knowledge (and a mathematical bent) or calling in an expert. All too often the accountant or other expert will report back that the investor's taxable gain is just inside the annual allowance so that there is no tax to pay – only the accountant's bill.

The personal equity plan investor should consider himself lucky to be able to avoid such calculations and to avoid needing an accountant too.

PEPs can be run only by officially approved managers
The investment business has attracted at least its fair share of rogues in the past. During 1988 the Financial Services Act is being implemented to require all investment advisers, including those selling and managing PEPs, to belong to bodies officially recognised by the government. In addition, however, PEP managers will have to be authorised by the Inland Revenue.

The investor can chose a PEP allowing him to select his own shares or one whose manager makes the choice
The investor insisting on choosing shares for herself or himself can do so, though this is unlikely to be a novice investor. The alternative is to use a PEP whose manager decides which shares to invest in: as PEPs are offered by managers such as stockbrokers, banks and investment companies, the new investor may feel that their judgement

in finding potentially profitable shares is better than his or her own. If nothing else, handing this function over to the manager means that the investor need not be worrying about whether his own decisions were wise or fearing that he has missed an opportunity known only to those professionals working full-time in investment markets.

The investor's life assurance company and pension scheme similarly accept his money and make the investment decisions for him, but PEPs differ in that the PEP manager must allow investors to know what shares he owns and what dividends they have paid. There must also be the opportunity for a PEP investor to receive the same information from a company that other shareholders in that company would, and to vote alongside these other investors when the company puts an issue to shareholders.

Personal equity plans allowing the managers to make the decisions are known as discretionary schemes; those where the investors retain control of the selection are non-discretionary.

PEPs can be invested in by anyone aged over 18 who is resident in the United Kingdom for tax purposes
This includes what the Inland Revenue also defines as 'ordinarily resident' and is different to being domiciled in the UK. Anyone who has spent their whole life in Britain or Northern Ireland can assume that they are ordinarily resident; anyone who comes to the country permanently is resident as soon as they arrive. Complications arise only for people who split their time between the UK and other countries. A foreigner who frequently visited the UK, spending over three months a year here for several years, might be regarded as resident by the Revenue. A Briton who spent a whole year overseas might well be regarded as non-resident. Most people would already have established or be arguing about their residency status with the tax authorities before investing in a PEP, but for those with a choice of where they are resident, it would be necessary to weigh up the tax liability of being resident in the United Kingdom against the tax saving of thus being permitted to put money into a PEP. If the choice is between a lower tax

rate abroad, then the decision would usually be to take it and to forfeit the PEP's advantage.

Certain non-resident investors, in particular Crown employees officially serving abroad, can still invest in personal equity plans.

A resident who does start a PEP but who emigrates will not forfeit the tax advantages that they had while they were resident here. They will not be able to put any further sums into their PEP, and they will not be able to start a new PEP while they are non-resident, but the investment which they have already made will be permitted to continue accumulating free of all taxes in Britain.

2 WHY ARE PEPS SO GOOD?

Personal Equity Plans invest in shares but the dividends and capital gains remain tax-free. Given that the average share has a very low dividend – about 3 per cent of the price paid for it before deducting income tax was typical before the 1987 crash, up to 4½ per cent immediately afterward – and that most people do not pay capital gains tax, it is tempting for a lot of readers to wonder what is so good about PEPs.

This chapter aims to demonstrate that PEPs offer gains for everybody, even if the gains are greatest for those who normally suffer the most tax. If some of the chapter seems a little complicated then do not worry; think of PEPs like a television set or similar appliance. It is not essential to understand how it works so long as one is confident that it does, and that one understands how to use it.

Firstly consider a comparison of shares with a building society investment. It must be emphasised again that these are two very different investments, but for many investors the decision to put money into shares is a decision not to put the same money into a savings account.

Although building societies offer 'share accounts' paying interest, these are not the same as shares in companies bought through stockbrokers or other agents – shares quoted on the stock market can fall in value; money put in building society share accounts or deposit accounts will not lose its capital value unless something disastrous happens to the society (and even if that did ever happen, there are compensation schemes to ensure that the saver does not lose totally). The effects of inflation may reduce the purchasing power of the capital, but in absolute terms, £100 put in a bank or building society will always be worth £100, and the balance will increase only if interest is left to roll-up inside the account.

Building societies or banks pay interest on investments made with them. That rate of interest may vary up and down but there is little doubt that a payment will always be made. In contrast, a company pays dividends to investors which own its shares. That dividend comes from profits, and profits are the difference between the revenue that the company earns and the costs of providing the goods or services supplied for that revenue.

A small rise in costs or a small fall in sales can reduce profits considerably or eliminate them. Companies can continue paying dividends from past reserves, and in good times they do not usually pay out their whole after-tax profits, preferring to build up those reserves. But it is by no means certain that a company will pay a dividend or that it will pay as much as in the previous year.

A company nevertheless hopes to increase its dividend in most years, and throughout the 1980s profits have risen at such a rate that many companies have been able to increase their dividends significantly. It is not unusual for one year's dividend payments to be 15 per cent more than the previous year's.

It is because dividends rise that investors are prepared to accept such an apparently low initial yield from shares. As said above, a typical share might have a dividend equivalent to 3 per cent. It is not the companies that are mean in paying such a low rate though: it is investors who force up the price of a share so that the company's dividend represents such a low yield. If a company pays a gross dividend of 3p a year that would be a 6 per cent return if the shares cost 50p but is only 3 per cent if demand from investors pushes up the share price to 100p. That 3 per cent would be worth just 2.19 per cent to most people though after basic-rate income tax has been deducted, even though a building society can offer a 10 per cent gross equivalent rate, which would be worth 7.3 per cent after tax.

Even for the PEP investor who does not have to pay

income tax on a company's dividends, 3 per cent is clearly less than the taxed interest from a building society. If that 3p dividend is increased at 15 per cent annually though, investors will receive 3.45p a share the next year, 3.97p the following year, 4.56p in the year after that and by the eighth year will be receiving 7.98p – which is more than the same money in a building society would be paying if the society's rate was still 7.3 per cent net. After ten years the share's dividend would be 10.55p compared with the 7.3p interest that a society could be still paying on £1 invested a decade beforehand, and from then onward, the shares' income would widen even further from the static or relatively static building society interest.

However, if that was the only advantage of a PEP and it required eight years of dividends below the income that a savings account pays, it would be hard to be enthusiastic about PEPs, never mind directly-held shares whose dividends are taxed.

One other advantage of PEPs and directly-held shares is that they should show some capital growth too; a savings account can not. Yet again, it has to be emphasised that share prices can fall, but if a company could keep increasing its dividend like the one in the example above, it would be exceptionally unusual for its share price not to rise.

The original investor seeking a 3 per cent initial yield was prepared to pay 100p for the shares when the company's dividend was 3p because he or she considered that the company would increase that dividend. If, six years later, the dividend was about 6p (as it would be if it was increased by 15 per cent a year) then a new investor seeking a 3 per cent initial yield because he thought that dividends would continue rising would be prepared to pay 200p for the share – a 6p dividend on the 200p being 3 per cent.

In reality, the share price might not have doubled exactly, but it certainly should have risen. After ten years when the company's dividend is about 10½p a share an investor demanding a 3 per cent yield would be prepared to pay 350p; even if the investment climate had changed over the decade so that investors demanded 5 per cent, then a price of over 200p would still provide that with that dividend.

27

Over time and if profits and dividends can keep generally rising, there should be capital growth, therefore. For PEP investors that growth is tax-free, but even other shareholders who are liable to capital gains tax expect some growth in the long term.

The graph below nevertheless ignores any capital growth, however unlikely that scenario is over a long period – it does however look at the position of investors who are deliberately seeking income rather than growth and comparing their investment with a bank or building society return.

Even when typical shares pay dividends representing about 3 per cent of their market price, by careful selection it is possible to find shares paying a higher return. An investor seeking high-yielding shares could construct a portfolio of companies whose payments represent around 5½ per cent of their market price. Immediately after the 1987 crash, even 7 per cent was available. Again, it is not that payments are high, but that investors have held down the price of the share through lack of demand. Sometimes investors are worried about the company's ability to keep paying that level of dividends or doubt that the payment will be increased significantly; sometimes there are fears that the company's share price could be hit by bad news. Often the concern is misplaced – the market as a whole can occasionally be very slow to appreciate the stamina of even well-known firms. Such companies can find themselves with a cloud over their reputation in City terms, therefore. Tiny Rowland's Lonrho for many years paid a high yield because of City distrust and uncertainty of what the group would do next; eventually the City realised that what Tiny did next was pay more good dividends. Concern over Midland Bank's international problems, Barratt Development's timber-frame houses or Guinness' scandals left all those shares on high yields.

And if a share can be bought by a PEP investor with a dividend giving a 5½ per cent return and the payment increases at 15 per cent annually, it will be only four years before the income matches that of the savings account paying 7.3 per cent after basic-rate tax. After a decade the shares' dividend would be showing a 13 per cent return on the original investment compared with the 7.3 per cent still being paid by the bank or building society.

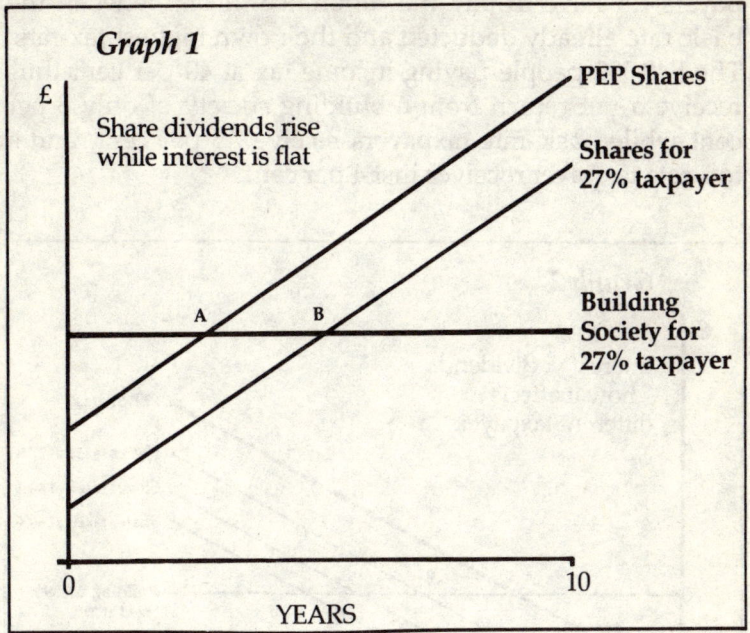

Graph 1

£

Share dividends rise while interest is flat

PEP Shares

Shares for 27% taxpayer

Building Society for 27% taxpayer

A   B

0   10

YEARS

Graph 1 shows how the untaxed PEP investor receives only 5.05 per cent initially compared with the higher savings account return, but how the PEP gives a better return from the fourth year. Point 'A' marks the crossover point. Had the same high-yielding shares been bought directly and basic-rate tax paid on the dividends, it would have been the eighth year before the taxed share dividends paid more than the taxed dividends, as Point 'B' shows.

Graph 2 shows those lines and points again, but adds in the position of a 40 per cent taxpayer – that is the first of the higher tax rates and in the tax-year ending in 1988 applies to any person or couple with a taxable income of over £17,900 – and for top-rate taxpayers who have 60 per cent of their taxable income above £41,200 deducted at that rate. These higher-rate taxpayers benefit more from a PEP than a basic-rate taxpayer because they save more by being permitted to receive dividends tax-free. They have to pay more tax than basic-rate payers on building society or bank interest too though: these savings accounts deduct tax at the basic rate so that most people have no further tax to pay, but high rate payers do have to pay the difference in tax between the basic rate already deducted and their own highest tax-rate. The 340,000 people paying income tax at 40 per cent thus receive a net return from a building society of only 6 per cent while basic-rate taxpayers receive 7.3 per cent, and a top-rate taxpayer receives just 4 per cent.

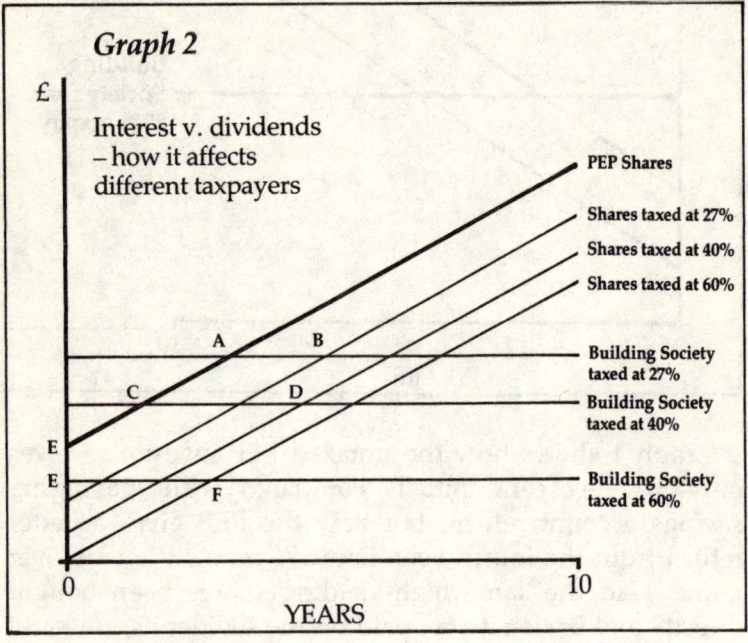

Graph 2

£

Interest v. dividends
– how it affects
different taxpayers

PEP Shares
Shares taxed at 27%
Shares taxed at 40%
Shares taxed at 60%
Building Society taxed at 27%
Building Society taxed at 40%
Building Society taxed at 60%

A   B
C   D
E
E
F

0   10
YEARS

The 5½ per cent untaxed yield from shares in a high-yielding PEP is only just below the interest that a 40 per cent taxpayer receives in the example at the very beginning. It thus takes only one year (or one 15 per cent increase in the shares' dividends) before the PEP shares are showing this taxpayer a better return than a savings account, as Point 'C' shows. Had the same investor bought shares outside a PEP it would have taken five years for the shares' dividends to outperform the interest, as marked by Point 'D'.

For the top-rate taxpayer, owning high-yield shares through a tax-free PEP gives an immediate return better than receiving bank or building society interest taxed at 60 per cent, as the difference between the two Point 'E's demonstrates. The same investor buying the same shares outside a PEP would have had to wait five years for a better return than the savings account – the same period as the taxpayers on other rates.

That shows how the annual income paid through shares in a PEP can be much better than dividend payment to non-PEP investors or to building society or bank savers. However, one of the conditions of a PEP is that dividends are paid back into the personal equity plan for re-investment rather than to the PEP investor.

This is the equivalent of a savings account whose interest is left in the account to roll-up rather than being paid directly to the saver, either by a regular cheque or into another of the saver's accounts such as a current bank account. If the interest is left in the account it adds to the balance, and in the next year the saver earns interest not only on the original investment but also on the interest left from the previous period. Similarly for PEP investors, the dividends received on shares in the plan can be used to buy more shares in the PEP, either in the same company or different ones. The income, whether dividends or interest, effectively becomes capital therefore when left in an account or PEP.

So while the previous two graphs showed the annual return from different investments for different investors, Graph 3 shows the effect of rolling up the income to increase the value of the PEP or savings account.

Each sum of £100 put in a building society offering the equivalent of 10 per cent gross interest and left there for a decade by a basic-rate taxpayer with the interest remaining in the account each year would have a balance of £202 after the ten years. The same amount of shares bought outside a PEP whose initial 5.05 per cent dividends are assumed to rise by 15 per cent annually and which are used to buy more shares would finish the decade with a value of just £185 if the shares themselves did not change in value. (Such a sum ignores stockbrokers' costs on the shares, which for a small sum would be considerable, but ignoring those costs, the shares' value would be the same 8 per cent below the savings account's whether the original investment in each was £100, £1,000 or £2,400. (In these examples a £100 base is used for simplicity.)

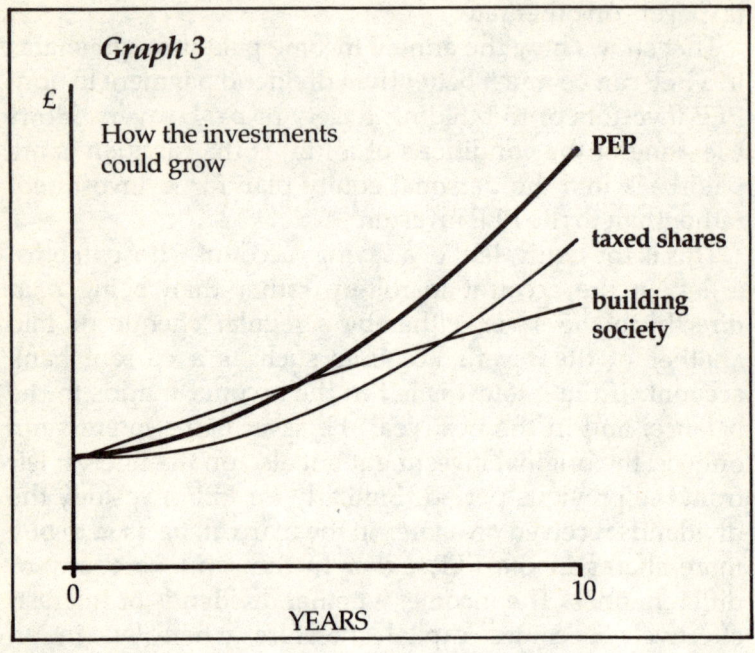

Graph 3

£

How the investments could grow

PEP

taxed shares

building society

0   10

YEARS

But each £100 put in the same shares through a PEP with the dividends re-invested would have a value after ten years of £231 on the same assumptions. The basic-rate taxpaying PEP investor thus has a 14.25 per cent advantage over the savings account, even without allowing for any capital gain.

Now let's look at what happens if some increase in share prices is built into the sums. The comparisons now are between buying shares inside a PEP and buying them out-side – not between shares and savings accounts. Graph 4 shows the rise in the value of typical shares which sell on the stockmarket at a 3 per cent yield, but whose share price does rise by 10 per cent annually. In recent years that would be both modest capital growth and a low yield. The graph also reflects the position of the majority of the population who pay no capital gains tax because their taxable realised gains do not exceed the threshold, which in the tax-year ending in 1988 was £6,600.

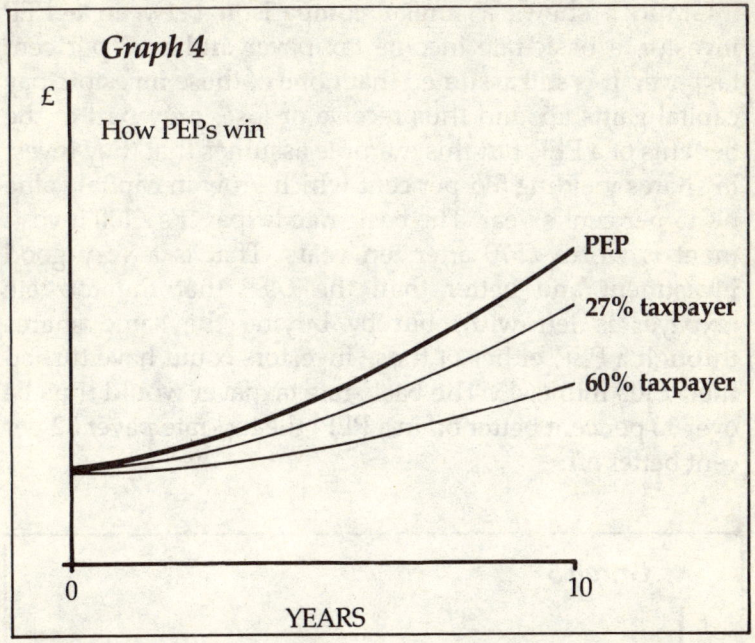

Graph 4

£

How PEPs win

PEP

27% taxpayer

60% taxpayer

0   10

YEARS

After the decade, this modest investment would have turned the PEP investor's £100 into £339 (which means £1,000 would be worth £3,390), while the basic-rate tax-payer's investment would be worth £315 and the top-rate taxpayer's £100 would have become £289. For a basic-rate taxpayer there is a 7.6 per cent advantage of using the PEP to buy shares, therefore; for the top rate taxpayer there is a 17.3 per cent advantage. That is only a small gain over a decade, but it is a real gain, and if there are no disadvantages of using a PEP to buy shares then it is worth using the personal equity plan. (Chapter 8 does spell out what disadvantages there can be in using PEPs: these are principally the charges, but the chapter points out how many charges can be avoided. Also, while these sums still ignore any costs of dealing in shares, the costs apply to both investment through PEPs and direct investment. Applying stock-brokers' and other charges would affect both PEP investors and non-PEP investors. The exactness of the numbers is not the important point of these examples; they do, however, show the degree of advantage of investing through a PEP.)

Graph 5 shows a similar comparison between a PEP investor, a basic-rate income tax payer and a 60 per cent taxpayer. It is still assumed that none of these investors pay capital gains tax and thus receive or lose, only part of the benefits of a PEP, but this example assumes that they invest in shares yielding 5½ per cent which grow in capital value by 15 per cent a year. The basic-rate taxpayer's £100 invest-ment is worth £570 after ten years. That is a very good investment and better than the £489 that the top-rate taxpayer is left with, but by buying the same shares through a PEP, either of those investors could have turned their £100 into £645. The basic-rate taxpayer would thus be over 13 per cent better off in a PEP; the top-rate payer 32 per cent better off.

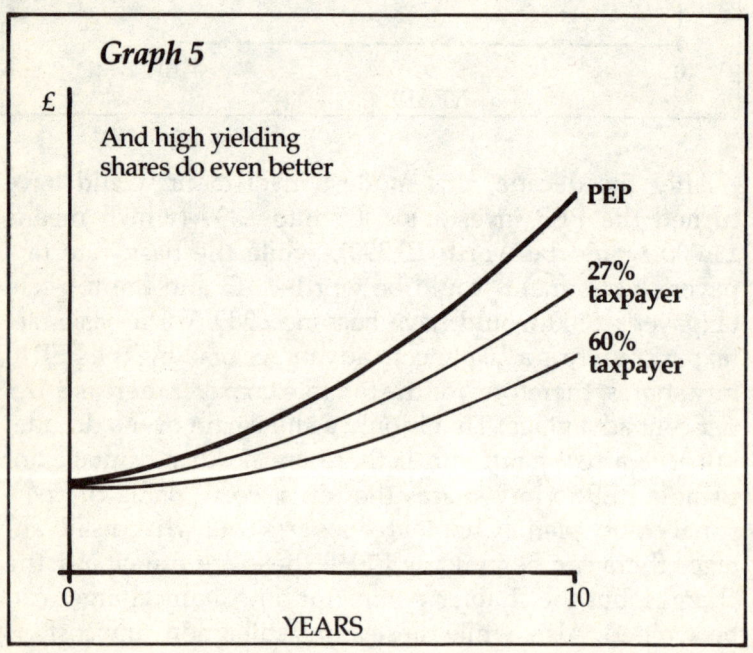

Graph 5

£

And high yielding shares do even better

PEP

27% taxpayer

60% taxpayer

0   10

YEARS

The next two graphs show the benefits of a PEP investment for a person subject to capital gains tax. Many of the people who think that this tax does not affect them may be surprised to find that it does. Simply because it has not had to be paid yet does not mean that the tax liability is not already stored up. For some people the biggest problem stems not from their shares or unit trusts at all, but from a second home they have bought. A cottage bought for a few thousand pounds a few years ago may not have seemed much of an investment then; with prices rising by even just 20 per cent a year as they have through the mid-1980s in most of the South-East, selling the property could easily trigger tax. After just five years of such rises (and gains have been much greater in some places) a £10,000 home would be worth nearly £25,000. Even allowing for inflation and certain costs, the taxable gain would be at least £12,000 – which is well over the exempt threshold. Capital gains tax on the cottage's sale would be about £3,500, therefore, but any other investment gains realised in the same year, such as shares, would automatically be taxed at the same 30 per cent rate. Do not forget that the annual exemption for realised taxable gains has to be shared between husband and wife.

Even people without second homes, or those who do not intend selling them, may still be caught by capital gains tax, however. Many share portfolios and unit trusts have appreciated by 30 per cent annually before 1987's setback. So £5,000 invested for four years would be worth over £14,000 on that basis; if it all had to be realised in a single year – say because the proceeds were required for a house purchase or because the investor foresaw a crash in stock markets or even because a cash takeover was received for the shares – then the capital gains tax threshold would be exceeded and any other gains realised would be automatically taxed.

And even those who have never invested £5,000 or any similar sum at any one time could still face capital gains tax. Simply by applying for the various privatisation share issues as they have been offered and by making relatively small investments (increased later in many cases when second instalments became due) many married couples could find themselves sitting on a potential tax liability if they still hold their shares. Staggering sales over different tax years should solve that problem, but that is not always an option open to investors.

Graph 6 shows the effect of investors buying shares yielding a high 5½ per cent but which also rise in value each year. It is assumed that the shares are sold at the end of each year for a price sufficient to give a 15 per cent gain after allowing for dealing costs – inflation of 4 per cent a year is allowed for in calculating capital gains tax liabilities. After a decade of such dealing, every £100 which the PEP investor starts with has turned into a £645 portfolio which is worth

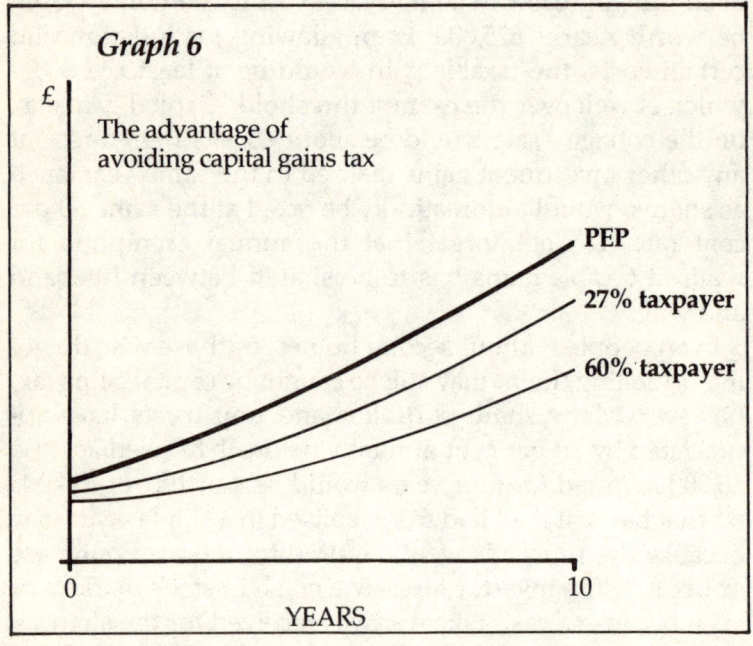

Graph 6

£

The advantage of
avoiding capital gains tax

PEP

27% taxpayer

60% taxpayer

0   10

YEARS

50 per cent more than the same shares held by a basic-rate income taxpayer who has been paying capital gains tax at 30 per cent too. The top-rate income taxpayer who also pays gains tax would have been more than 75 per cent better off owning the same shares through a PEP.

Graph 7 shows the different growth rates in the portfolios of the PEP investor, the basic-rate income taxpayer and the top-rate payer if by good luck or good management their shares rise in value by 30 per cent a year for the whole decade.

This would be exceptional growth, and no one should invest in a PEP in the hope that that will happen even necessarily for part of the decade. As can be seen, however, each £100 that the PEP investor subscribed has turned into £2,086 over the ten years – more than twice as much as the basic-rate taxpayer is left with after paying capital gains tax every time shares were sold each year. The PEP investor has done even better compared with the person paying 60 per cent income tax and 30 per cent capital gains tax.

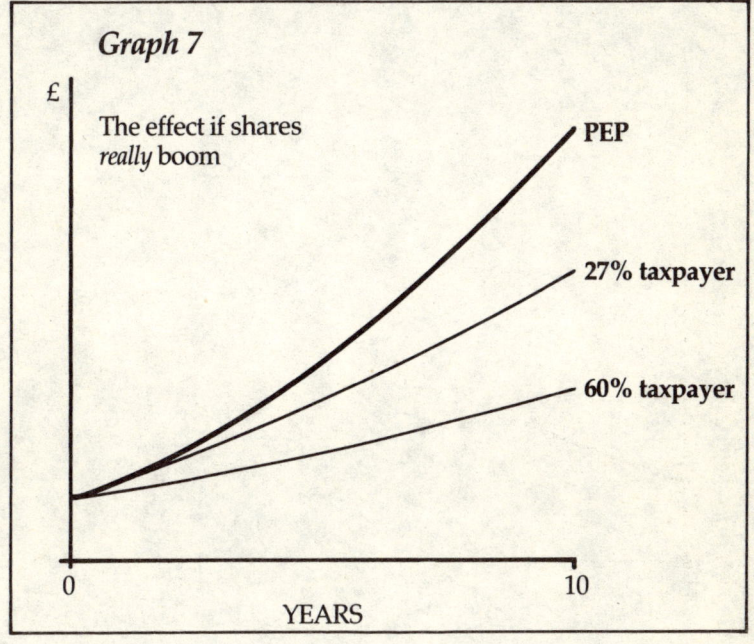

This final example of how a basic-rate taxpayer can double his or her money with a personal equity plan well demonstrates the effect that a PEP's tax advantages can give if share prices rise significantly. Even the previous example's 50 per cent advantage from a comparatively modest 15 per cent annual gain in share prices would not be scoffed at by most people.

3 HOW SAFE ARE PEPS?

All investment is a balance of risk and reward. That's why favourites in horse races have the shortest odds while the least likely winners give the greatest pay-outs if they do pass the post first. It's why most people still prefer to put their money in building societies, which have proved to be exceptionally low risk even though rewards are rarely even 10 per cent net annually, rather than stock markets where the scope for profits is far greater – but so is the risk of making no profit at all.

Much of the reason that investment in shares has increased considerably in recent years is because people have revised their perception of the balance between the risk and reward; after so many years of steadily rising share prices it was tempting to regard the chance of losing money as small until autumn 1987. The instant profits made by applicants for shares in British Telecom and more recent privatisations have suggested that the risks from shares are low too, and the backing which the government itself has given to share-ownership has no doubt led many to consider that the shares would not be being sold in such an official manner if there were any risk. This is not so. The novice moving for the first time from the relatively safe havens of a building society account into shares should realise that he is leaving the town for the jungle; the rewards can be considerable, and PEPs can make them larger still, but so can the risks.

A personal equity plan, as earlier chapters described, involves buying shares through a plan manager in British companies or unit trusts. The rewards are tax-free with a PEP, but what are the risks? Quite simply, the plan manager might be dishonest or incompetent so that your money is never even invested in shares; that the manager does invest it or deposit it, but in vehicles which are outside the PEP scheme so losing you your tax advantages; that the manager invests in valid vehicles, but ones which themselves are dishonest or incompetent; or that the money is invested in quite valid and competent vehicles, but simply ones which perform badly. To return to that horse racing analogy, you could find you have bet with a bent bookie, that you've put your stake on a nobbled horse – or simply that your horse loses.

It is sensible to consider the safeguards therefore which are intended to protect the investor from losing his money.

From 1988, no one in Britain is permitted to give investment advice or to manage investments without being authorised by one of a group of officially recognised bodies. The Financial Services Act makes it a criminal offence to carry on an investment business without being authorised. Whether a PEP is a discretionary scheme with the manager choosing the investments, or a non-discretionary scheme with the plan manager merely managing the investments, the manager must therefore be authorised.

Authorisation is given by either the Securities & Investments Board or one of five self-regulatory organisations which report to the board. Each of these bodies is supposed to ensure that companies and individuals are fit and proper and are not only competent and honest, but also that they have sufficient capital to support their businesses. Regular checks are made on members to ensure that their finances and their record-keeping are adequate, and there can be spot-checks too, though it has to be pointed out that membership of one of these bodies is no guarantee of probity – rogues can slip through the net, and previously sound members can become rogues.

The two self-regulatory bodies to whom PEP managers are likely to belong are The Securities Association, which includes all Stock Exchange members, and Fimbra, the Financial Intermediaries, Managers & Brokers Regulatory Association. There are also Recognised Professional Bodies which regulate solicitors and accountants, and a PEP manager could seek authorisation directly from the

Securities & Investments Board. Of the sort of companies offering PEPs, stockbroking firms would be authorised by The Securities Association, unit trust companies by Lautro and Imro (Investment Management Regulatory Organisation) with investment advisers such as insurance brokers authorised by Fimbra. Solicitors and accountants have their professional bodies; addresses are given at the end of this chapter.

Although the different self-regulatory organisations have their own rule books, they are written to incorporate the same principles and safeguards. Any complaint from the public of breach of rules discovered by regular or spot checks will first be investigated by the organisations' own officers. The Securities & Investments Board has a variety of sanctions ranging from private or public reprimands up to suspension of a firm's authorisation, or, if necessary, the termination of that authorisation.

There is also an arbitration system and an ombudsman covering each area of investment, plus the creation of compensation schemes to recompense investors suffering losses because of a firm's breach of the rules. The Securities & Investments Board will, if necessary, sue an allegedly miscreant investment manager or adviser on the behalf of a member of the public too. That latter point could be important to investors unwilling to commit themselves to high legal costs to recover what might be an investment of £2,400 or less.

Some investment organisations have operated compensation schemes in the past. The Financial Services Act ensures that all do from 1988. Normally recompense should come from the Securities & Investments Board suing the allegedly irregular PEP plan manager, or suing a fund manager whose unit trust or investment trust had been invested in by the PEP manager. If the managers, whether of the PEP or an underlying fund, have gone bust or are unable to afford to pay claims fully, then the compensation scheme is triggered. Schemes are operated by each of the self-regulatory organisations, but if any particular scheme is unable to pay out – say because of the scale of claims by a whole mass of investors – then the rest of the investment industry including those responsible to other self-regulatory organisations will contribute too.

Individual payments under compensation arrangements are limited to £48,000 – they are paid in full on the first £30,000 of loss, but with only 90 per cent of the next £20,000 recoverable – but with the PEP investment limited to £2,400 in any year, it would take some years and good growth from several different plans before even the £30,000 limit is breached.

Anyone who attempted to offer or to run a PEP without authorisation could be jailed for two years, and the requirements described above now apply to all investment managers. Personal equity plans offer certain further protections, however. It is necessary for all PEP managers to be registered with the Inland Revenue as well; the Revenue will itself check that prospective managers are eligible. And while some building societies will be able to operate their own PEPs, not all will – only those societies with assets of £100 million or more will be permitted to manage investments through PEPs themselves – smaller societies will be able only to market plans for other eligible managers.

And there are rules on what a PEP manager can do with cash given to him by the public before it is invested, or cash received from the sale of shares. A plan manager such as National Westminster or Lloyds Bank who is authorised by the Bank of England to take deposits can look after the cash itself; other managers such as most stockbrokers and financial advisers must put all cash into a segregated account at an authorised bank, and the investor must be credited with all interest due. At least once a year the manager must tell the investor how much cash he or she holds in the plan.

Further, the cash must be held in sterling, not in dollars or yen or any other currency. There is no prospect of it losing its value because of fluctuations on foreign exchanges therefore. And just in case the authorised bank runs into financial problems, investors do still have the same compensation arrangements as if they had placed the cash in an account of their own; at least 75 per cent of any deposits up to £20,000 are guaranteed by the Bank of England.

If a PEP manager intentionally or accidentally breaches any of these controls his authorisation to be a manager can be removed. Investors need still not worry unduly however – their tax advantages and their investments need not be lost – there are provisions for the personal equity plan to be switched in its entirety to a new PEP manager with all the trigger dates continuing to run unaffected. The procedure is described more fully on page 72, but the investor's loss should be limited to no more than a possible administrative charge, a delay during which it might be difficult to withdraw cash even if the investor wanted to, and to being forced to accept a plan manager which was clearly not the investor's original choice.

There is one further provision which should both ensure that plan managers do not run off with PEP customers' investments and which should help investors sleep more soundly. The investor remains the beneficial owner of all shares in a PEP, even if these are usually held jointly in the names of the plan manager and the investor himself.

But however sound the PEP manager, there remains the risk of the investors' money being put into unsound investments. It is fairly unusual now for companies with Stock Exchange quotations to be put into receivership leaving the shares valueless, but that is only a recent phenomenon. Even in the mid 1980s the Stock Exchange became used to a series of regular announcements from companies seeking a suspension of dealing in their shares pending 'clarification of their position' – a euphemism preceding the appointment of receivers, and later liquidators. A hundred pounds or a thousand pounds in such companies as engineers Acrow and Alfred Herbert or toymakers Dunbee Combex Marx and Airfix, typically became worth nothing, and had the shares been inside a PEP there would have been no comfort for the investor that dividends or capital gains were tax-free, because there would be none.

But if shares do not frequently lose their whole value nowadays, there are plenty of examples of shares which plunge in value so that £1,000 invested is worth perhaps only half that by the end of the year. Even while the stock market is climbing steadily higher, individual shares can fall in value. After the Guinness scandal was revealed, shares in the brewing company fell from over 300p to 263p, while shares in its merchant bank Morgan Grenfell plunged to 353p, even though the bank had been floated on the stock exchange over six months earlier at £5. After another seven months, takeover hopes lifted Morgan Grenfell's shares back above that £5 for the first time, and three months later the 1987 crash knocked them back below 220p.

There is no guaranteed way of picking winners in the stock market – or even of avoiding shares whose price takes a sudden tumble. There is little comeback on an adviser who recommends losers either. This chapter has described the action which an investor can take against his investment manager if the firm is dishonest or incompetent. Incompetence would cover an adviser failing to invest money in a PEP before the end of the calendar year, so depriving the customer of a year's tax benefits; it would not include a firm which bought Guinness shares before their fall. Had PEPs been operating then, such a purchase would have been regarded as quite reasonable at the time however wrong it proved later. Indeed, that balance between risk and reward mentioned at the beginning of the chapter means that the companies most likely to perform spectacularly well can also be the ones most likely to do badly too.

The investor has three ways of reducing the risk of investing in a PEP whose shares perform badly. Either apparently 'safe' shares can be chosen, even though their performance is not expected to be startling; managers with good records and investment skills can be selected; and the PEP can invest in a wide range of investments to spread the risk.

Later chapters will give some guidance in choosing shares and managers – the spreading of risk is something which can be mentioned here. Investors have probably not got all their eggs in one basket at the moment. A typical reader may have part of his wealth in his house, part in a building society or bank, part in his pension or life assurance policies. His or her car may be of some value too, and the house may contain a few antiques. If the market for antiques turns sour, then at least the house should keep its value, and the money on account should be safe too. The investor has thus spread his risk.

The managers of those pension schemes and life policies spread the investor's risk further by splitting his money between government gilt-edged stock, property and shares, and spread it further still by investing in more than one company's shares and probably companies abroad as well as in Britain. If the investor also owns unit trusts he will have a spread too. Although a trust may concentrate on a specific investment sector – say Japan or small companies – it will probably buy shares in several dozen companies in that sector.

The PEP investor can use exactly the same basis for spreading his risk by using his sum of up to £2,400 to buy shares in not one company, but many. There is no restriction on the whole amount being used to buy just one firm's shares, but the majority of PEP managers who are offering discretionary plans will themselves be seeking to put their customers into at least a handful of different shares. There are restrictions on what shares can and cannot be bought, and that does to an extent limit the breadth of spread that can be offered, but the manager can put at least part of the PEP money into a unit trust or an investment trust which itself may be invested in several dozen shares – that way even a small sum of little over £400 can be very well spread, not only among different British companies, but companies around the world.

Of course the investor not using investment or unit trusts, and especially the investor choosing his own shares through a non-discretionary PEP, will find that even the full £2,400 cannot be spread too widely without it being spread thinly and possibly incurring high stockbrokers' dealing costs, but the breadth of the spread should take into consideration all the shares that the investor may hold outside of his PEP too.

A wide range of shares can help balance out the rises at some companies with the falls at others, but it will be of less help when the whole stock market follows a general trend.

The trend has been very clearly upward from 1979 until the advent of PEPs eight years later; October 1987 proved how suddenly trends can change.

Investment in Japan or America or other countries through investment or unit trusts may give some protection against falls in the British market alone, but there can be times when markets all over the world fall – indeed a fall in one can trigger slides in others. Shares are risk investments, and PEPs are investments in shares.

Self-regulatory organisations

Financial Intermediaries, Managers & Brokers Regulatory Association
22 Great Tower Street
London EC3R 5AQ

Investment Management Regulatory Organisation
Centre Point
103 New Oxford Street
London WC1A 1PT

Life Assurance & Unit Trust Regulatory Association
Centre Point
103 New Oxford Street
London WC1A 1QH

The Securities Association
The Stock Exchange
London
EC2N 1EQ

4 WHAT CAN I INVEST IN?

If an investor decides to put money into a personal equity plan – whether the full £2,400 in a year, or a lesser sum – it can be invested in either cash, shares, or into a unit trust or investment trust which itself invests in shares. There are strict limits, however, governing how much can be in any of those categories at a particular time.

Cash

When the investment is first made into the PEP the money will be in cash. It could be turned into shares the same day – though such is the nature of share buying that it is usually at least a week before payment has to be made – or the cash could lie there either until a manager is ready to invest several peoples' PEP investments or until a suitable buying opportunity is spotted.

The cash will thus earn interest, and this interest will belong to the individual PEP investor and will accrue without tax being deducted. Normally, bank or building society interest is paid with basic-rate income tax deducted and with an obligation for higher rate taxpayers to pay the difference too.

There is virtually no risk with the cash investment, of course. The capital deposited cannot fall in value (though inflation might erode its spending power); it ought to be deposited with a deposit-taker recognised by the Bank of England, and there will be a Bank of England compensation scheme offering the return of at least 75 per cent of the principal if the deposit-taker did default. The cash has to be deposited in sterling too, so currency fluctuations cannot alter the money's value. For the investor who is averse to risk, therefore, the PEP offers what is effectively a tax-free bank account with virtually no possibility of loss. The capital gains tax advantage of a PEP cannot be employed, because there will be no capital gain on a cash deposit, but for a person with a high marginal income tax rate, the opportunity of receiving interest free of income tax is considerable. A 7.3 per cent return paid after basic-rate income tax by a bank or building society is the equivalent of 10 per cent gross, but is normally worth only 4 per cent to a top-rate 60 per cent taxpayer – put another way that taxpayer would have to have received 25 per cent from elsewhere to be left with the 10 per cent gross he can receive inside a PEP.

The bank or building society or deposit taker with whom the cash is deposited has the authority to pay interest without first deducting tax, so there should be no delay while tax is reclaimed from the Inland Revenue.

Some readers may recognise such an arrangement as being akin to the 'roll up' funds which became very popular in the period up to the end of 1983 – when they were effectively restricted because of their success. These funds were based offshore, usually in the Channel Islands, but were run by well-known London names, frequently merchant banks. They allowed interest to roll up into capital; when the interest was brought back to Britain it was taxed – but as a capital gain rather than as income. For the majority of savers who were not utilising their annual capital gains tax allowance, the interest could be brought back to Britain tax-free therefore; for high-rate income taxpayers it was still better to pay 30 per cent gains tax even if they had used up their tax allowance, than to pay a higher income tax rate. Despite the similarities though, there are some distinct differences between interest in a roll-up fund and interest in a PEP. Firstly, there is no capital gains tax with the PEP for anyone; secondly it is not necessary to go offshore; thirdly a PEP is much less flexible. The tax advantage is lost if the cash is withdrawn prematurely, and there is a limit to how long cash can remain in a PEP before it is converted into shares or unit trusts.

The key dates with PEP plans are January 1 and December 31. A PEP must run for a complete calendar year from the start of January to the end of December to qualify. An investor could put money into a PEP on December 31, 1988 (if anyone would accept it on a Saturday) and need leave it there merely for that day and the following year to qualify for the tax advantages; or he could have invested it on January 2, 1988 (another Saturday) to spend all of that year in the PEP, and all of 1989 in the PEPs before it would qualify for the tax advantages.

It is the investor's choice, but while in either case, for the second period – the clear January to December year – most of the money must be invested in shares or units, it can remain completely in cash for the period up until the calendar year starts on January 1. So it is during this first period before the clear year that the advantage of tax-free interest can be exploited.

If investors were wary about the stock market, or indeed could see it falling sharply, they could remain in cash for as long as was considered prudent during this pre-January 1 period. Even if their money had been used to buy shares or units, they could be sold and the proceeds left in the PEP as cash again.

But once the calendar year starts, no more than 10 per cent of the previous December 31's PEP value – or £240 if that is greater – can be held in cash for more than 28 days. So if those limits are exceeded because shares or unit trusts are sold, the PEP manager has to purchase new investments within four weeks. If the PEP manager has kept the plan very liquid during the period before the January 1 start of the qualifying tax year, most of the money will have to be invested by January 28.

If this 28-day rule is broken during the qualifying tax year the whole PEP becomes invalid. If the rule is broken in subsequent years the excess cash has to be withdrawn and interest earned during the whole of the tax year (not the calendar year as is usual with PEPs) will be subject to income tax. If any withdrawals are made, the figure for

49

calculating the 10 per cent ceiling is adjusted by that amount. So if the December 31 balance was £4,000 and £1,000 was withdrawn in the following June, the PEP could keep £400 in cash until June, then £300. If another £1,000 was withdrawn, leaving £2,000, the £240 cash limit would apply.

Shares

As explained above, almost all the PEP-holder's money must be invested within 28 days of the first January 1 date being passed, though it can be completely invested before that date. The rules of personal equity plans allow it to be invested in unit trusts or investment trusts (but with considerable limitations which are discussed below) or in shares of companies other than investment trusts, which are quoted on the Stock Exchange. These companies must also be incorporated in the UK, which means that their registered offices must be somewhere in Britain or Northern Ireland and that they must file accounts complying with UK law to Companies House in Cardiff, Edinburgh or Belfast.

There are more than 850,000 companies registered in the United Kingdom, but only a small proportion have their shares quoted. Many of the companies are owned by each other: Ever-Ready Ltd is wholly-owned by Hanson plc for instance, Dorothy Perkins' shares are owned by Burton Group and Berni Inns' by Grand Metropolitan. Many of the companies are private, owned by one person or family – a local garage or shop, for instance. A few are large with quite a number of shareholders but have not – or not yet – sought to have the shares listed on a Stock Exchange; Littlewoods the pools and shops group is one example. There are a number of advantages of a Stock Exchange listing, one of which is that it provides a daily market for people to exchange shares, which in turn gives a daily price for the shares enabling other investors to value their own holdings. It is not an advantage which every eligible company seeks, but there are nevertheless more than 2,400 shares quoted on the London Stock Exchange, and almost all can be bought through PEPs.

Even though Ever-Ready shares cannot be bought, for instance, those in its parent company, Hanson can – as can the shares of other well-known names such as ICI, Barclays Bank or Ladbroke Group, plus those of much smaller and less famous companies. Not quite all companies quoted on the London Stock Exchange are acceptable as PEP investments though; IBM the computer company, for instance, has a quotation, but as it is registered in New York, it does not qualify. Some British-based companies including Hanson do have share quotations in Paris and Switzerland and New York as well as London, but that does not affect their acceptability for PEPs. The London Stock Exchange has a 'junior division', mainly of smaller or newer companies, called the Unlisted Securities Market, but although this is technically distinct from the rest of the Stock Exchange, shares quoted on this USM qualify for PEPs too so long as the companies are UK-registered.

There is also a third market operated by the Stock Exchange – an even more junior version than the USM. The small number of shares quoted on this market do not qualify for inclusion inside a PEP, however, and neither do those shares quoted on 'over-the-counter' markets.

Unit trusts and Investment trusts

Investment trusts are companies which own shares in other companies, usually in several other companies. Although the trust's own shares are for most purposes treated exactly like any other company's shares, they are treated differently for investors wanting to put them into PEPs. Investment trust shares can be put into PEPs with their capital gains remaining totally tax free and their dividends remaining free of income tax, but there are restrictions. These restrictions apply to unit trusts too.

Unit trusts are not technically companies, but they too are funds which invest in a wide variety of other companies' shares. Again, unit trusts can be put into PEPs, and the capital gains and dividends received from them remain tax-free, but there are constraints.

Most notably, it is not possible to put a person's maximum £2,400 annual PEP investment into either unit or investment trusts. Only £420, or a quarter of the year's PEP money if that is greater, can be put into a trust. Someone investing all £2,400 could put £600 of that into these trusts therefore; someone investing £1,200 could put £420 into trusts because that is more than a quarter of the total. For any investment of £1,680 or less, the £420 maximum applies: larger total investments permit a larger amount to go into unit or investment trusts – but never more than the £600.

The other main restriction involving these trusts means that unless PEP money is used in the first instance to buy units or investment trust shares, the PEP cannot later invest in the trusts. If a PEP investor's cash is used to buy investment trust shares or units in a unit trust, these can be sold subsequently with the proceeds used to buy more units or investment trust shares.

Alternatively, the trust investments could be sold and the proceeds used to buy ordinary shares in other companies. However, if those shares were then sold, the proceeds could not be used to buy back into unit or investment trusts. Similarly, PEP money which had originally been invested in ordinary shares can never be re-used to buy into these trusts. There is effectively a one-way valve which prevents money in shares later being invested in unit or investment trusts. The investor wanting to maximise his or her holding in these trusts must buy the largest permitted amount at the start of the personal equity plan therefore and not let the holding fall; proceeds of any sale would have to be used to buy more units or investment trust shares. Investments in unit trusts can be transferred into investment trust shares, however, and vice versa.

What is so good about investment trusts and unit trusts that they have to be restricted, a cynic might ask. The government argues that the restriction is there because they do not give the PEP investor first-hand experience of share-owning – the investor merely holds a stake in a vehicle which owns shares. But there are a number of distinct advantages of owning shares through a trust which are unavailable with direct holdings. Firstly, each single trust holding gives the investor a stake in the shares of a wide range of companies – usually at least a couple of dozen. One trust thus gives the spread of risk that an investor ought to have. Secondly, both unit trusts and investment trusts are permitted to invest in overseas companies – indeed many specialise in the companies of one particular region or country. The trusts thus give an opportunity to share in the fortunes of companies that could not be bought directly through a PEP because they are not incorporated in the United Kingdom or have no Stock Exchange quotation here.

Further, by investing abroad in this way, the PEP investor's fortunes can be related in some way to foreign currencies. This introduces an element of risk, but it can work profitably for the investor. A share quoted in New York at $10 may still be worth $10 a year later, but if the pound's value against the dollar has slipped from $1.70 to $1.50 over the year, the sterling value of that share has risen from £5.88 to £6.66, giving a gain for the UK investor in a trust, which was not available to the American investor – and not to the PEP investor buying shares directly because it was not an eligible share.

And because all investment trusts and unit trusts are run by professional managers, the investor using a trust is obtaining a degree of skilled management; the investor does not have to decide which share to buy or sell, or have the trouble of doing the transaction, the management company uses its expertise to do it for the investor. There is a charge for providing that management, but that is paid by all investors in these trusts, whether or not the investment is made through a PEP. Charges are discussed in Chapter 8.

There are more than 1,000 unit trusts registered in Britain. Many are managed by companies whose names are probably well known – Save & Prosper, M&G or GT, for instance. Many are managed by names which are well known, though possibly for services other than their unit trusts – the Prudential insurance and estate agency group, for instance, merchant bank N M Rothschild, or stock-brokers James Capel. Some trusts are large with investors' funds of more than £400m; others own less than £1 million of shares. Some buy only shares in British companies – ones which a direct PEP investor could have bought himself: others invest in countries all over the world, and still others specialise in companies in just one country such as Spain or Japan. Some trusts specialise by industry, just shares in property companies or leisure businesses, for example.

The degree of risk varies, depending on the degree of specialisation and the particular market in which the trust operates, and the investor should appreciate that while, say a German unit trust offers a wide spread of German companies, its own price is vulnerable to the whole German stock market falling – or to the deutschmark weakening against the pound. The trust can protect its investors against adverse currency movements however, by 'hedging', but at a cost.

Unit trusts do have a lot in common, however. The fund is divided up into the number of units held by investors; if more investors want to participate, new units can be issued to them. New investors can be advertised for, and weekend newspapers often carry advertisements for a considerable range of trusts. The price of the units is a mathematical division of the value of the shares in the trust by the number of units; a rise in the sterling value of the trust's shares will automatically cause a rise in the unit price therefore. Unit prices are calculated daily and quoted in major newspapers such as *The Daily Telegraph*. The units can be bought and sold freely through financial advisers or from and to the management company with nothing more than administrative delays. There is no charge for buying or selling, but the units do have an 'offer' price at which investors buy and a lower 'bid' price at which they sell – the difference paying the costs of the transaction.

Some characteristics of investment trusts are similar to unit trusts. A trust invested only in German shares again offers a spread of risk beyond one company but is still vulnerable to a move in the whole German market, or a move in the currency unless it too 'hedges'. An investment trust is a company whose own shares are quoted on the stock market however, and while normally a fall in the value of the shares in the investment trust would cause its own shares to fall, there is no mathematical link. The trust's own shares, like any other shares, are priced at a level determined by the pressure of buying and selling in the market.

New shares cannot easily be created to meet demand from investors. And although a mathematical calculation can be made of the net asset value of each investment trust share – the value of the trust's investment less any borrowings, divided by the number of shares – this is not their price.

An investment trust has the power to borrow, or gear-up, too: in rising stock markets this has the effect of turning a small rise in the shares owned by the trust into a larger rise in the trust's own asset value, though when stock prices fall, the downward effect on the investment trust's worth is even greater.

Traditionally, trusts' stock market share prices have been below the calculated net asset value, though the size of this discount varies at different times: when stock markets rise, this discount works in the investor's favour too – though in falling markets it works against him. Like unit trusts, investment trusts receive dividends from the companies in which they have invested: all or part of these payments are passed on to unit holders or shareholders in the investment trust, though normally with income tax deducted at the standard rate. In either case, PEP managers can recover this tax for their investors, just as they have to for any shares in other companies which they have bought for the PEP.

The merits of investment trusts compared with unit trusts have often been argued. For the purpose of personal equity plans they are treated the same – which means less favourably than other shares.

There are nevertheless some common investments, many quoted on the Stock Exchange, which do not qualify at all for PEPs.

Gilts, prefs, debs, loan stocks, options and futures

The government's own gilt-edged stock is quoted on the Stock Exchange, but it cannot be held inside a PEP. Although PEP investors are allowed to keep at least part of their investment in cash, giving a safe capital with a tax-free income, the government is not prepared to extend that privilege to owning its own stock. The capital value of the stock does in fact move up and down on the Stock Exchange, but any gains made are free of capital gains tax anyway: it is only from the dividends that PEP investors are deprived by the exclusion of gilts.

Preference shares, loan stocks, and debentures are private enterprise versions of the government's gilt-edged stock, a quoted capital unit paying a fixed annual income but whose price can move up or down. Like gilts, they do not qualify for PEPs. Even those loan stocks which can at some date be converted into the shares of a company whose shares would normally be eligible for a PEP do not qualify.

While a PEP cannot buy these stocks directly, it can invest in a unit trust which itself invests in gilts, preference shares and similar vehicles. The amount of PEP money that can be put into units is limited, but there are a number of unit trusts which specialise in these fixed-interest stocks.

Indeed, while a gilts unit trust is a poor investment because it can involve paying capital gains tax on the units' gain in value when the gain on gilts themselves is tax-free, PEPs make the gain on the units tax-free again.

Options and futures are ways of gambling on the anticipated movement of the market price of an investment, including ordinary shares. While the shares themselves may qualify for PEPs, the options and futures do not.

Gold, property, ships, oil-wells, antiques, diamonds, stamps, etc

Gilts, prefs, debs and the investments in the paragraphs above are at least Stock Exchange investments, but ones which do not qualify for PEPs. Investments not listed on the

Stock Exchange certainly do not qualify. There is a wide variety of exotic and alternative investments, but they are not for PEP investment. PEP investors can, however, buy shares in companies which own gold mines or office blocks or tankers or whatever, but not the assets themselves.

5 HOW DO I CHOOSE A PEP?

The investor interested in a personal equity plan should first decide whether to have a non-discretionary plan which the investor manages and chooses the investments for, or to have a discretionary PEP whose manager makes the decisions. The choice is then between shares and unit trusts or investment trusts. The non-discretionary PEP investor will have to make the choice of which shares or which units. There is also the choice of investing small regular amounts, or a single lump-sum. Next the investor should consider which plan managers will provide the best service including administration – and then what the costs are.

Discretionary or non-discretionary?

My choice or theirs?

Most of the PEPs on offer are from managers who are offering to be investment managers as well as administrative managers. They want either to select their own range of shares for the investor or to put the investor into an existing unit trust which they are already managing. A small number of PEP managers offer non-discretionary plans, however – where the investor has the discretion to choose how the plan invests.

If an investor is to choose a non-discretionary plan, he or she should have either a good source of investment advice or faith (preferably backed up with some proof) in their own investment abilities. If the investor makes the wrong investment decisions it is not only the money which could be lost, but the opportunity to invest through a PEP in that calendar year. It is better to lose money outside a PEP and let an expert make it inside for you, than for the expert to manage your non-PEP funds well, while you make losses in the personal equity plan.

Stockbrokers running a non-discretionary PEP will be willing to give some limited advice on the shares to include, but many brokers will be running their own discretionary PEP and may well try to divert clients into that. Some investors have successfully run their own portfolios for years using either skill in analysing under-rated shares or reading tips in newspapers or other publications; some have simply been successful because the stock market was rising anyway. This chapter will later discuss the different sorts of investments which investors may want to consider if they choose a non discretionary PEP; most relatively novice investors will prefer to leave the management to someone else, however.

Discretionary PEPs

Plans run by discretionary fund managers can invest in either shares, unit trusts or a mixture. To some extent the investor has the choice – because managers tend to indicate in advance what their policy will be – though the manager may retain the freedom to switch between trusts and shares. The manager also has another choice: to keep money in cash.

For the period between putting the investment into the PEP until the January 1 when the tax-qualifying calendar year starts, the whole investment can be in cash, after that only 10 per cent of the previous year-end's balance, though that limit can be exceeded for up to 28 days. There may be occasions when it was thought wise to be exceptionally liquid for those 28 days, or even once that initial qualifying tax year is complete, to exceed the limit and consequently lose the tax relief on what interest was earned during that year. (Confusingly, income tax has to be paid on interest earned from PEP cash in the tax-year to April 5, in those unusual circumstances, not the calendar year which is otherwise the crucial period for PEPs.) If investors' money is to remain in cash, it is sensible to check what interest rate will be received or what sort of account it will be held in: the manager can receive interest gross, so do not compare his rate with the lower after-tax rates quoted by banks and building societies.

Some PEP managers invest money only in unit trusts, and thus limit investors to a maximum £420 instead of the £2,400 which can otherwise be put into PEPs. It is not possible to start a second PEP with another £1,980 to stay inside the limit either: only one PEP is permitted. For the investor with more than that available, it would be limiting to select a manager with such a restriction.

Some PEP managers invest in shares as well as unit trusts to enable customers to utilise their maximum allowance, but insist that the maximum permitted element does go into units. These are usually unit trust companies whose main aim is to enhance sales of their own units. Inevitably, the only unit trusts available are those managed by the PEP managers.

One of the advantages of using unit trusts at all is that they can give an international aspect to the PEP which is not obtainable with directly held shares, as well as a broader range of shares because the trust itself invests in 30 or more different stocks.

Investing in an existing trust allows investors to check the fund's track record too, which may help him or her decide whether it looks a sound investment. Unit trusts are generally good vehicles for new investors, and unit trust investment through PEPs is similarly sensible for the relative novice. Investors may not be offered a management company's complete range of unit trusts however; check therefore that what is on offer meets your own requirements.

For the element of the PEP which goes into shares of the managers' choosing, there may again be a choice from only a limited range – say, from the 100 companies' shares which constitute the *Financial Times'* and Stock Exchange's joint FTSE 100 index of prices, or a choice from a smaller range of 'blue chip' shares in large companies. These will almost all be familiar names. Managers will construct a portfolio – possibly indicating in advance their objective or its likely breadth – which balances security with potential growth. Investors should look for any indication of whether the managers will attempt to seek high income, high security, high capital growth or whatever. Reading the section below on non-discretionary PEPs, while intended for investors making their own choice of shares, may help concentrate discretionary PEP investors' minds on the sort of shares their own managers could be or should be looking for.

Prospective investors should also consider what expertise the PEP manager has in selecting shares. Although all managers have to meet certain requirements to be regis-tered as managers, they do not have to prove that they are capable of managing a portfolio. Some PEPs are managed by companies which have access to potential clients, some by companies with systems that can handle the necessary paperwork – and some by firms which have experience of selecting profitable investments.

A PEP managed by a stockbroker should have some ability to identify attractive shares. A fund management group – which could mean a unit trust company or pension fund manager – is also in the business of selecting shares which should prosper: it too ought to be capable of identi-fying situations, and of providing smooth administration.

Many of the PEP managers' names will be well known to investors – National Westminster Bank, the Prudential or Save & Prosper, for instance. They have reputations to maintain, but that may restrict them from attempting to invest in some of the more obscure shares which could prove to have exceptional growth. Often these are shares in very small companies and a PEP manager with a large number of investors could not hope to secure sufficient shares: a PEP managed by a small stockbroker with fewer clients may be able to buy such shares, however.

Non-discretionary PEPs

The investor who is confident enough to run his own portfolio through a PEP can tailor-make his investment much more closely than the people buying off-the-peg PEPs from discretionary managers. If the investor pays no capital gains tax, for instance, and has no fear of doing so, and particularly if the investor pays income tax at a high rate, it is possible to use a PEP to receive dividends from a company at their gross rate – even though the dividends received by the PEP do have to stay inside for a short period at least.

Unfortunately, the Inland Revenue declines to say how long dividends should stay inside a PEP before being withdrawn for this not to be regarded as an abuse of the scheme. But investors with this objective should seek high yielding shares to maximise their dividends. The quality newspapers' daily lists of share prices also include the shares' yield and investors can run their fingers down the lists looking for any figure of, say, 5 per cent or more. Omit those high-yielding shares which are loan stocks or preference shares or other ineligible investments though, and do seek some corroborating evidence that a particular stock is a potentially sound investment.

There can be advantages or disadvantages in buying a share at a particular time too. Unlike building societies which, despite calculating savers' interest once or twice a year, actually pay interest all year (so the total interest payment reflects how many days the investment was held in the account) shares usually pay dividends only on two days of the year. So whoever is registered as owning the share on one particular date receives the whole dividend for the first half of the year, and whoever is registered as owning the shares on a second particular date about six months later will receive the whole of the final dividend. A long-term investor might own the shares on both dates, and he or she would see the price move at the time of the relevant dates to reflect the fact that new investors are no longer buying with the right to receive the payment and would have to wait six months or so for another.

The price of a share with the right to an imminent dividend will be higher than the price would be without the entitlement to that payment – the difference reflecting the net dividends expected. PEP investors receive the payment untaxed however, so for them the extra price paid for the shares should be more than compensated for by the dividend. There is an advantage therefore in buying a share shortly before a dividend is due.

Final dividends are usually larger than interim dividends too. They are often twice the size, so that is a better dividend to buy before. The Inland Revenue will not give relief on what it considers 'dividend washing' – repeatedly buying before dividend payments and selling afterwards but keeping the untaxed dividend – but any investor is best advised to take what advantage of this phenomenon is possible. Unfortunately again, the Inland Revenue will not say how persistently a PEP holder could perform such purchases and sales before relief is withdrawn, but an investor looking for income would be foolish to buy a share just after the date that registered holders receive a dividend. All other things being equal it is much better to buy just before the date – the actual size of the payment will usually have been announced already.

Not all investors are seeking high yields, however, and although the shares pay an income to the PEP, the PEP cannot pay an income to its investor until withdrawals are possible after the first full calendar year. The investor making his or her own choice can select shares from any particular favoured sector, such as shares of oil companies or textile firms or property groups. It is impossible to discuss the merits of particular sectors here in any more detail than an investor considering a non-discretionary PEP should have already, but clearly some sectors are more intrinsically stable than others, some are more susceptible to currency movements or international trade and some are affected more than others by rising commodity costs or rising labour costs.

The investor is free to exercise private prejudices too. Shares in a company he or she does not like can be avoided; indeed, the investor can construct a personal portfolio to parallel the 'ethical' unit trusts now offered by a number of groups – funds which invest only in companies deemed to be clean in the sense that they are not involved in, say, armaments, alcohol or tobacco. The investor is of course free to construct a totally unethical portfolio of every immoral company he or she can think of too.

In running a portfolio personally, the investor must take on much of the responsibility for ensuring that he does not transgress any of the complicated rules governing PEPs. If, for instance, during the PEP's first calendar year, more than 10 per cent of the previous December 31's investment value is held in cash for more than 28 days, the whole plan becomes void. A sharp eye is required therefore.

Charges

Chapter 8 deals in detail with the different charges that can be imposed on PEP managers. Briefly, however, investors should check what they are being charged for and whether it is excessive. There may be some very expensive charges on a particular PEP, but if they are not ones which will affect you, do not be put off; it might even be that those charges are subsidising the low charges that you will pay.

Check whether any annual management charge is imposed on the element of their investment which remains in cash. As cash requires very little investment skill compared with shares, there should be very little cost – or better still, none.

Check too whether there is double charging for money invested in unit trusts. Unit trust managers impose an annual charge and a front-end charge, as do most PEP managers. Some PEP managers waive or reduce part of their charges to avoid the investor paying twice.

Look at what the PEP manager charges investors wanting to attend company meetings. Some of these charges are horrendous – but if you do not want to attend meetings then there is no need to pay.

Consider too the penalty charges imposed on investors wanting to withdraw their money from a PEP prematurely. Although it is probably unlikely that you will start a scheme and change your mind, at least bear in mind the cost. Some groups also charge for withdrawals made after the first tax-qualifying year is complete. Given that you presumably want to withdraw the money at some time, that cost will have to be borne ultimately.

Regular or lump-sum?

Not everyone has the choice of whether they invest each month or in one go: not everyone has enough money to make a lump-sum investment. Not all companies offer the choice either: many accept only lump sums, and only for specific amounts – usually £1,200 or £2,400, either the full allowance or half of it.

A lump-sum made when the PEP is started clearly gets the whole investment working for the investor immediately, giving more of the tax free benefits. It might be that the whole sum was invested in the market at the top, however, and that for the following months, share prices tumbled. In that case it would have been better to put the whole sum into the PEP later when prices were lower – but if investors are uncertain what markets are doing in the short term (and they cannot rely on PEP managers to tell them *whether* to invest) then splitting the investment would be wise; some of the cash might be invested at a good price and some at a bad price, but it is better than getting the whole investment wrong.

The unit trust industry has a history of accepting regular investments from customers which it uses to buy units at the price prevailing each month when the cash is received. There is no attempt to decide which months are the best opportunities for investing – the same amount is put into the units regardless of their price. The units industry argues the virtue of this practice, which it calls 'pound cost averaging'. When unit or share prices are high the regular £100 or whatever buys £100 of units, but relatively few units. Although the investor suffers on that investment if the price falls, the fall means that the next £100 instalment buys more units than the previous £100 did. If the price recovers therefore, there is a greater number of units to benefit from the recovery.

The same 'pound cost averaging' argument can be

applied to money put into PEPs to buy shares, but if the investor believes that a market is rising steadily, it will always be better to make a lump-sum investment as early as possible.

PICK YOUR OWN

ENJOY THE FRUITS OF THE MARKET.

NatWest PEPs are a flexible way of obtaining TAX FREE income from investing in shares in British companies.

The NatWest PEP Plan allows you to pick your own shares from the thousands of British companies listed on the stock market. And within the Plan, sell and buy when you choose. Remember shares can go down as well as up.

ALTERNATIVELY you can leave it up to NatWest investment experts to select shares on your behalf.

EITHER WAY NatWest take care of the paperwork, leaving you free to enjoy the fruits of the market.

 **National Westminster Bank PLC**

For an application form and the NatWest PEP brochure make a free phone call to 0800 400 474 or write to Margaret McAlpine, National Westminster Bank PLC, NatWest PEP Office, 11 Old Broad Street, London EC2N 1BB.

6 WHAT HAPPENS AFTER THE FIRST YEAR?

The first important date for a personal equity plan is December 31. Investment in a PEP has to be made by then so that it will be there for the whole of the following calendar year so that the income and capital gains from the shares remain tax-free, not only for that year, but for the period before it started, and after that key qualifying year ends.

The next important date is the following December 31; after then cash can be withdrawn from the PEP by taking dividends or selling shares, and the tax advantages will not be lost. It is necessary to wait for more than a year therefore before benefits can be reaped from the PEP that could not have been obtained by investing directly in shares or unit trusts.

PEP holders should not rush to cash in their year's worth or two years' worth of profits though. Unless they desperately need the cash, it is sensible to keep the PEP going. What investors can now do is to keep for themselves the dividends received from the shares or units inside the PEP – but investors will be subject to income tax on their payments. Better therefore to allow these dividends to continue being paid to the PEP gross – the full untaxed amount could then be withdrawn later without there being a tax penalty. Unfortunately the Inland Revenue will not say whether investors who persistently withdraw an amount of cash equal to their dividend payment as soon as that payment was received by the PEP would be abusing the scheme and in danger of forfeiting their tax relief.

Remember too that some PEPs charge for cash withdrawals, even when the qualifying tax year is complete.

After that qualifying tax year is complete, the investor could have the shares in the PEP transferred out to be held directly by the investor too, but again, from the moment of transfer, there would be a potential liability to capital gains tax on all profits made after the transfer. If the investor is merely going to retain the shares it is better to leave them inside the PEP. Although one complete calendar year is necessary for a PEP to receive the tax concessions, these benefits do not end after that year. Money left inside the PEP can continue accruing free of income tax or capital gains tax forever, or at least, until Parliament orders a change in PEPs' current rules. That is why the examples of possible growth patterns in the previous chapter looked at what could happen over ten years.

A PEP is deemed to be 'mature' once this initial tax-qualifying year is complete. By the time a plan is mature, however, the investor may have two other PEPs in earlier stages. Let us say that the mature plan had been started sometime in 1988. So long as the money remained in the plan during the whole of 1989 it would have qualified for the tax benefits. In 1990 it would be a mature plan. But in 1989 the investor could have started a new PEP whose qualifying tax year would be 1990. And in 1990 the investor could have put new money into another PEP which had still to start its qualifying year. Families which have produced home-made wine will probably recognise the cycle: some fruit being prepared, some fermenting, some bottled and ready for drinking.

By 1991, however, the investor's second PEP started in 1989 will be mature too. Although the three PEPs and their portfolios must be kept separate when they are in their pre-qualifying, qualifying and post-qualifying periods, mature PEPs can be consolidated. That means that portfolios can be merged, so that larger deals can be made, which should lower dealings' costs, and means that the combined PEPs can be more flexible in use of the cash restrictions. It is less likely that one PEP reaches its cash limit while another is still well below if the two PEPs are put together. Besides cutting costs, combining mature PEPs means that the investor will receive less paperwork and less duplicated paperwork.

This can happen only if all the maturing PEPs have been taken out with the same PEP manager. If the investor has bought different PEPs through different managers, however, there is no loss. The PEP holder will merely find that he or she receives more paperwork from the variety of managers than had the different years' PEPs been amalgamated.

The rules affecting what a mature PEP can invest in are no different to the rules applying during the qualifying tax year. Shares must still be in quoted British companies and unit trusts are restricted to their original maximum. However, while cash above a specific limit must be re-invested within 28 days during the qualifying year or the whole PEP becomes invalid, a breach of the 28-day rule in a mature PEP merely requires the excess cash to be withdrawn from the PEP. That is a penalty, however, because money taken out of a PEP can never be put back in.

Cash in a PEP only as a last resort

A mature PEP can be cashed in without penalty, but the investor should do so only if desperate. While the amount of cash invested originally may possibly have doubled or appreciated even more, making it tempting to use the capital, remember, that taking money from a PEP cancels a tax benefit irredeemably. On present limits, £2,400 every year can be put into a PEP. If the investor in, say, 1992, withdraws £4,000 from a PEP started in 1987, then there can be no more tax-free dividends or gains from that money. If in 1993 the investor wants to put the £4,000 back into a PEP it will be impossible if the annual limit is still £2,400, and the investor may have already started a PEP for that year. Even if a past PEP has performed poorly it is worth continuing. All future gains on what is left of the amount invested in the PEP will remain tax-free. If you think it has performed poorly because of bad management (possibly by yourself if it is a non-discretionary PEP) consider transferring it to a new manager.

There are, of course, times when it is sensible to realise investments – that is why they are made, and there is no point saving for rainy days if the money is not used when it does pour. People moving house may require the accumulated capital in their PEP. Parents facing school fees may specifically have started PEPs each year to provide the fees as they fall due annually. But if an investor has a choice of realising shares in a PEP or realising shares held outside, it will almost certainly be more sensible to realise the ones held directly where no tax advantage is lost (though some capital gains tax may be due). If it is a choice between selling shares or units in a PEP, or withdrawing cash from a bank or building society account, the investor must weigh up the effect it would have on his or her overall portfolio and cash position. If finance must be found and the alternative is to surrender a life assurance policy or national savings certificates, then it may be that losing a PEP's

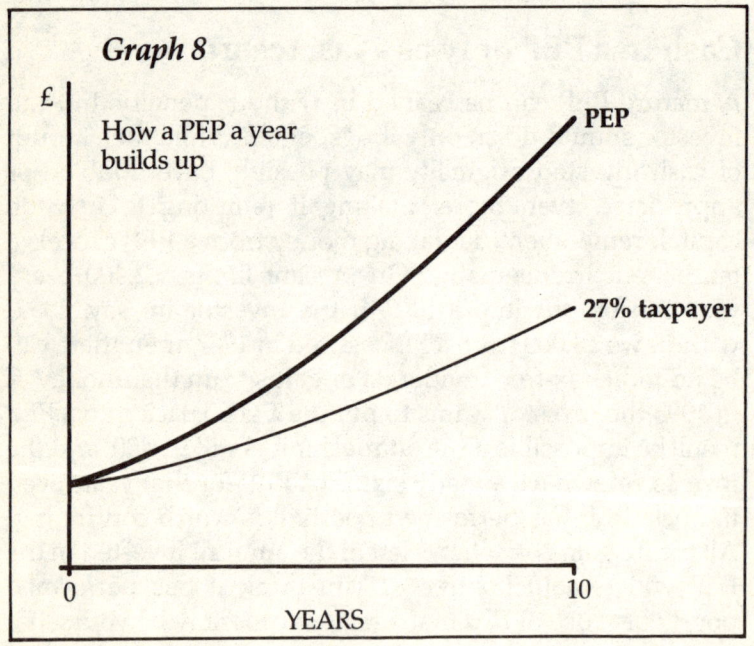

Graph 8

£

How a PEP a year
builds up

PEP

27% taxpayer

0   10

YEARS

advantages is a smaller loss than losing the other investments' benefits. Chapter 10 discusses how PEPs compare in tax efficiency with other investments.

Let this chapter conclude with one more graph. The figures of Graph 6 in Chapter 2 showed how each £100 invested in shares with their 5½ per cent yield re-invested and appreciating at 15 per cent a year would be worth £430 at the end of a decade to a basic-rate income tax payer liable to capital gains tax when the shares were sold each year and the proceeds re-invested. Inside a PEP, each £100 invested in exactly the same shares would have turned into £645.

If every year the investor kept putting £100 into a PEP which bought those shares the total investment would be worth £3,206 after a decade, compared with £2,433 for each £100 invested annually in the same shares outside a PEP. And if the maximum £2,400 had been invested annually the PEP investor would end the decade with £76,950 for a £24,000 investment – whereas the non-PEP investor's money would have turned into less than £58,400. Little acorns grow into oak trees, but the PEP is a very effective fertiliser.

7 WHAT IF I CHANGE MY MIND? WHAT IF I WANT MY MONEY BACK?

There is no point putting money into a PEP if one day it cannot come out. And in case the day when the proceeds are required comes sooner than anticipated, it is useful if there is a means of realising the investment prematurely. Given that dividends and interest earned by the PEP investment must stay inside the personal equity plan, some ultimate realisation becomes essential if the PEP holder is to benefit from his investment.

Investors generally have become used to being able to realise certain investments quickly. Building societies used to offer accounts which required seven days' notice to make a withdrawal, or 28 days or 90 days, with interest rates rising fractionally to compensate for the longer withdrawal periods. Now most money in building societies can be withdrawn immediately from no-notice instant-access accounts or accounts that offer that facility so long as balances stay above a particular level. There are still accounts for which notice has to be given, but even then there is now usually the alternative of having the money now and paying a penalty. Shares bought in new issues such as British Telecom or Rolls-Royce can be sold almost instantly if the new shares have not yet been registered, with the stockbroker sending a cheque within days of receiving the selling instructions. Other share sales take slightly longer but a cheque should usually follow within three weeks of asking the stockbroker to sell. Selling a car might be possible today if it is taken to a local dealer but will almost certainly take longer if it is advertised in a local newspaper. Receiving the proceeds from a house sale can take months.

There are occasions when we need cash, either temporarily or for the medium term, and we have to consider which of our existing investments to realise. Building society savings are often the easiest to dip into – indeed, that is why they are there. For items such as holidays it may be decided to sell shares, either because that is the readiest form of cash, or because a sale was being contemplated anyway. Often the expenditure has been anticipated, such as for school fees: occasionally it is unexpected, as when the central heating packs up or the car breaks down. Sometimes more drastic realisations have to be effected and for longer term expenditure, such as finding the capital to top-up the price being paid for a new house. It is no use then having good capital tied up in a PEP if it cannot be taken out.

Any money in a PEP can be taken out, with what should usually be only a slight delay, but there are likely to be other disadvantages for the investor besides the wait.

If the investor changes his or her mind before the crucial calendar year starts – that is before the first January 1 which comes after he or she commences investing in the PEP – then the money can be returned, but all the tax advantages associated with the PEP will be lost. If the investment had remained in cash during that period the interest earned will no longer be tax-free once the money, or any part of it, is withdrawn. If all or part had been used to buy shares or units in a trust, then the dividends received will no longer be tax-free once a withdrawal is made. And any capital appreciation in the value of the shares or units will be potentially liable to capital gains tax too, though the investors will still have their usual allowance of over £6,000 annual realised gains and the usual indexation provisions will allow the effects of inflation to be offset. In other words, if any money is withdrawn from a PEP in the period before the complete calendar year commences, the PEP becomes invalid and all income and capital gains are taxed just as if they had never been part of a PEP. The plan manager will deduct the tax before returning the investment to the investor, and the manager must give details of how the capital gains tax liability can be calculated. The onus for paying any gains tax due rests with the investor himself, but details of the investment will have been given by the plan manager to the Inland Revenue.

And if money is withdrawn from a PEP during that initial period, it is not permitted to put new money back into the PEP later, even if the £2,400 maximum would not be breached.

Even in the first crucial calendar year during which investment has to remain in the PEP for it to qualify for the tax advantages, no withdrawals can be made either, and the dividends or interest arising from the investment must stay within the PEP rather than be paid to the PEP holder too. Again, any withdrawal, however small, would invalidate the whole PEP and leave the investor having to pay tax on the income or capital gains. And again, after a withdrawal, money cannot be re-invested in a plan.

After the first calendar year is complete, however, withdrawals can be made without past tax advantages being lost. And the advantages are allowed to continue for that year up until the date of the withdrawal; it is not necessary for investments to remain in a PEP for complete calendar years once the first calendar year is finished. It is not necessary to withdraw the whole PEP investment; only a small part can be taken out or only a small part left in, but the investor still cannot put money back into that PEP, despite the withdrawal. What is more, if a complete or partial withdrawal is made from a PEP once the first calendar year is complete, the plan manager need not inform the Inland Revenue of the withdrawal or of what investments are left inside the PEP.

So if a PEP was started in June 1988, any withdrawal before December 31, 1989 would make the whole PEP invalid. From January 1, 1990 all or part of the investment – which the investor will hope has increased in size during that period – can be withdrawn with all tax benefits dating back to June 1988 remaining intact. If the withdrawal was in June 1990, there would be two years' of benefit. But if the withdrawal left, say £1,000 in the PEP, the investor cannot put any new money into it to top it up to £2,400 or any other level. It is a 1989 PEP, and from January 1 that year it is closed for new investment. The investor is free to invest in a new PEP for 1990, but the money for that would already have had to have been invested by the end of 1989. In 1990 it is possible to invest in a PEP for the 1991 calendar year only.

For the investor subscribing a regular monthly sum who changes his or her mind, it is again impossible to withdraw funds without making the PEP void, but the option is open not to put any new money into the PEP, leaving the past investment to roll up tax-free.

If an investor does decide to withdraw from a PEP he does not have to take cash, however. It is possible to request that the shares held in the investor's name inside the PEP are given to him to hold directly, and the plan managers must hand over the shares, plus any cash, if requested. The tax advantages are lost if this withdrawal is made before the end of the PEP's first complete calendar year, as described above, but after that year is complete, the capital gains and income remain tax-free for the period up to the withdrawal, though from then onward, the investor will have to pay tax on any interest or dividends received after the withdrawal, and on the capital gain accruing above the value of the shares or units at the withdrawal date. The plan manager must inform the investor of the value of the investments at the date of the withdrawal to help the investor calculate any capital gains tax due when they are eventually sold.

Withdrawing investments from a PEP does not need to involve losing the tax benefits though. All PEP subscribers have the right to transfer their investment from one PEP to another. A PEP plan manager must allow the investments to be transferred out in this manner, though no PEP manager is obliged to accept a transfer into his scheme. All tax advantages will continue in such an instance as though the PEP had run from its original date with no transfer.

Investors might want to transfer a PEP because they were unimpressed with the investment performance of their original choice of manager, or because that manager's charges seemed high relative to another firm's. A transfer would be the only alternative to ending a plan, however, if the plan manager for any reason chose to go out of business or was forced to cease practising – possibly because his registration had been revoked by the Inland Revenue or authorisation to deal or advise had been revoked by one of the self-regulatory organisations created by the Financial Services Act. A manager who did lose his authority to continue managing PEPs is obliged to inform the investors of that fact and to ask whether they wish to have their investments transferred, or if they would prefer to terminate their PEP.

There may be a further penalty to closing a personal equity plan besides losing tax advantages though. Some PEP managers make a charge.

Full details of charges are given in the tables at the back of this book, and charges are discussed in Chapter 8. Paying to retrieve one's own money is not something that many people enjoy though; a plan manager making a charge should only be chosen if that particular plan has other compensating features.

8 WHAT ARE THE SNAGS? WHAT DOES IT COST?

Easy money is never earned easily. If the government is giving away tax, as it effectively is with PEPs, there have to be some snags. And, of course, there are. To translate the Yorkshire saying, you get nothing for nothing.

If tax concessions are PEPs' main advantages, then the main disadvantage is that it is necessary to tie up capital for at least several months to obtain those concessions. Earlier chapters described how money had to be in a PEP for at least a year and a day to qualify and not just any 366 or 367 days. It must be from before January 1 one year to at least the end of December that year. June 17 until June 18 the next year will not do; a June 17 investment would have to stay in a PEP until December 31 the following year to qualify.

There are other inflexibilities in the system too – no partial withdrawals before that second December 31 is reached; only a limited sum in unit trusts or investment trusts and no money re-invested from shares into those trusts; only certain shares, and only so much cash. Earlier chapters have described more fully those restrictions.

The other complaint that PEP investors are likely to have is that they have to pay for their PEPs. Some PEP managers make an initial charge when the investment is first made; almost all levy an annual charge; some, as mentioned in Chapter 7, impose a penalty on investors leaving prematurely and some even make a charge for leaving after the qualifying tax year is over. And a number of PEP managers demand extra payment if investors want to attend the annual meetings of companies in which they own shares.

On top of that there are all the normal stockbrokers' dealings charges that have to be paid every time a share is bought or sold, plus a tax payable to the government (technically stamp duty to the Inland Revenue) on every purchase. PEPs are not entirely tax-free therefore. With investments in unit trusts there can be additional initial charges and annual charges too, though the stamp duty and stockbrokers' dealing costs are currently built into the unit trusts' pricing structure. It may seem now that the investor will be lucky to see any of his own money back again once everyone else has taken their slice; the section below looks at who is asking for what from your PEP.

Unit trust charges

Irrespective of whether investors put money into a unit trust through a PEP or directly, they will find that the trust managers impose two charges – an annual fee plus an initial fee. It is like paying to join a club as well as having to pay the annual subscription.

Initial charges

All units and all shares have two prices, one at which they can be bought and one at which they can be sold. Not surprisingly, the investor has to buy at the higher of the two and sell at the lower. With shares, the difference is retained by the Stock Exchange market-maker – a sort of shares wholesaler – to cover his costs. At present with units this spread, as the difference between the prices is known, covers both that difference between the buying and selling prices of the shares actually in the trust, the stamp duty payable to the Inland Revenue when the trust buys shares, and the trust managers' costs and profits. The spread on shares varies with popular shares usually having the smallest difference between buying and selling prices, but the spread between a unit trust's bid and offer price is currently usually about 5 to 6 per cent. And that 5 to 6 per cent usually includes a specific fee which the small print of the unit trusts managers' advertisements or other documents calls an 'initial charge'. This charge, sometimes known too as a front-end load or up-front charge is typically 5 or 5.25 per cent and covers any commission paid by the unit managers to a financial adviser who may have recommended that his client buys the units. So if £100 were invested it would immediately be worth only around £95, even before the unit price rises or falls over the days. Put another way, the investor has to see the unit price rise by around 5 per cent before he can sell at a bid price which repays the offer price that he paid.

There are proposals to change this wide spread of prices which includes the initial charge into a small spread – but for the initial charge to be levied separately. The net effect is unchanged and will be more like the practice of buying shares on a thin spread but having to pay the stockbroker as well.

Annual charges

Having taken part of your money when you enter the unit trust, the unit trust managers then impose a charge each year, also based on the value of your investment – though now they also share in any increase that there has been in the price of your units because the annual charge is a proportion of the value of the holding after every six or 12 months. Annual charges vary, but 0.75 per cent is now unusually low; 1 or 1.25 per cent is much more common – and the government imposes value added tax at 15 per cent on those annual management charges. The investor who put £100 into a trust and saw its redemption value fall immediately to £95 would find it worth another £1 or so less after a year if there were no change in the actual bid or offer prices and no dividend had been paid.

Both annual and initial charges are inevitable with unit trusts and the investor buying units through a PEP is not paying the unit managers any more than had he invested directly. Where he or she can lose out, however, is that some PEP managers then impose a further initial and annual charge of their own on top of the charges made by the unit trust companies. In some cases, however, the unit trust manager is also the PEP manager, so it is the same company taking the two fees.

PEP initial charges

The initial charge imposed by some PEP managers is a fee levied to cover the costs of establishing a PEP in addition to the fees that will be taken for running the PEP. Not all managers demand an initial fee though, and some of those who do effectively absorb it into the initial charge which there is on unit trusts which they invest in, so their investors do not pay twice. But while there is only one initial charge when a PEP is opened (though further charges if further PEPs are started in subsequent years) initial charges are paid on unit trust investments every time units are bought. If money was put into, say, a unit trust investing in American shares there would be the 5 per cent or so initial charge; if those units were later sold and the proceeds used to buy into a Japanese unit trust, there would be a second initial charge. Frequent switching between unit trusts can erode the capital, therefore, but if the switch is between trusts managed by the same company, there is often a discount, reducing the subsequent initial charge to around 3 per cent.

Yorkshire Bank has no up-front charge on its PEPs while the Prudential makes no initial charge other than that taken on the part of the investment it puts into unit trusts, and the Bank of Scotland has no front-end charges on its shares-only PEP. Most other schemes claiming to make no initial charge do so only because all the money is put into unit trusts which do have a charge.

Of the PEP managers who do make initial charges, the method varies. The Bradford & Bingley building society's PEP, for instance, imposes a charge of 5 per cent on the money being put into the personal equity plan and the government then imposes 15 per cent VAT on the 5 per cent charge. So £1,000 put into the PEP would require a further £50 payment to the managers and £7.50 VAT on that £50, a total of £1,057.50, though only £1,000 goes into the PEP. It is for that reason that some managers can claim that the maximum investment into its PEP is £2,538 rather than the £2,400 mentioned frequently in this book – £2,400 would go into the PEP, £120 to the managers, and £18 to the VAT man.

But many PEP managers invest the money which they receive into unit trusts, and that means incurring that other 5 per cent up-front charge as well as the manager's initial charge.

Some other PEP managers charge a flat initial fee whatever size investment is made. Brown Shipley, for instance, demands £36 (plus the inevitable value added tax) while fund managers Framlington on its partly-units PEP, and stockbrokers Kitcat & Aitken, both ask for £75 plus VAT.

PEP annual charges

Most – but not all – personal equity plan managers impose an annual charge for running the plan and to cover the costs of keeping the investor informed about his or her investment. Again, this can be additional to the annual charge made on holdings in unit trusts. In most cases the annual charge is a proportion of the value of the portfolio in the PEP assessed either annually or half-yearly. The typical fee is 1.25 or 1.50 per cent of the valuation each year, usually including any cash element (plus VAT on that fee), though a few managers impose a flat charge.

The Alliance Trust's is one PEP scheme which has no annual charge, but all the money goes into an investment trust, which effectively has its own annual charge built into its share price to remunerate the managers.

PEP managers charging lower than average annual fees include the Bank of Scotland on its units-only PEPs with 0.75 per cent, though it also imposes the unit trusts' own charges. Fund managers GT and bank Brown Shipley charge 1 per cent a year, but only on the part of the PEP invested in shares, not the unit trust or cash elements. A few managers impose a £10 or £15 minimum fee in case the percentage calculation on small investments would give them less than that. Some charge £15 or £20 fixed charges instead of a percentage.

If they are best-buys on annual charges, then the high

charging PEP managers include National Westminster Bank's 2 per cent on share-only PEPs, the Prudential's 2 per cent and FS Investment Managers' 2.4 per cent.

The tables later in this book give full charging details, and clearly it is worth avoiding the high charges. Remember though that the tax-saving on dividends received is worth about 1 per cent for most people and that if capital growth of an extra 5 per cent can be achieved by a good manager, it is worth paying him an extra 1 per cent or so for it. But there are other charges too.

Share dealing costs

Every time the investments inside the PEP are swapped around it costs the investor money. Only cash can be moved with no cost. This chapter earlier explained that there is a 5 or 6 per cent loss when a unit trust is bought because of the difference between bid and offer prices. There are, however, no costs involved in buying those units. A similar loss or cost has to be borne when buying shares to cover the difference between the price at which the shares are bought and their selling price, but there are also costs to pay to the stockbroker for buying the shares. The spread between shares' bid and offer prices is typically only 1 or 2 per cent on popular shares, but with the 0.5 per cent stamp duty payable to the Inland Revenue on all purchases (not just purchases over a certain value as with the stamp duty on house acquisitions) and the brokers' costs plus more brokers' costs when the shares are sold, the total can be similar to the 5 or 6 per cent of unit trusts.

Investment trusts are for dealing purposes akin to other shares, even though PEP rules link them with unit trusts in limiting the use that PEPs can make of them. Though investment trusts have fund managers selecting and dealing in shares of other companies, just as unit trusts have, the managers' costs are not levied separately on investors as with units, but are absorbed by the investment trust, so lowering its profits and its ability to pay dividends. The investor does pay for the management therefore, but the cost is reflected in his income and in the share price. But when investment trust shares are bought, there is the 0.5 per cent stamp duty which unit managers absorb into their initial charge, and there are the stockbroking costs as well as the spread between the investment trust's bid and offer price. And while there are no costs involved in selling unit trusts, investment trust sales incur a further set of stock-brokers' charges.

Anyone who has bought or sold shares outside of a PEP will already have encountered brokers' charges – and possibly have been surprised at their size. A standard commission for dealing is 1.65 per cent of the value of the shares being bought or sold (plus VAT on that), but there is often a minimum fee, which in recent years has typically increased from £10 to £20 or so. A £20 fee would be 4 per cent of a £500 transaction. Most PEP managers are charging less than that, however – and in particular, most have no minimum dealing fees.

Like annual charges, most are a percentage of the trans-action value, but a few PEP managers are charging flat fees. Stockbroker Hoare Govett, for instance, charges a flat £3 plus VAT per sale or purchase, brokers John Siddall charge £5, and the Alliance Trust investment trust charges just 50p. Stockbrokers Neilson Milnes have a £20 charge – and brokers Rensburg charge nothing. The 1.65 per cent is demanded by fund managers Perpetual, stockbrokers Laurence Keen, Kitcat & Aitken, Alexanders Laing & Cruickshank and some others. More typical pro rata fees are .25 to .50 per cent, but do not forget that that has to be paid on purchases as well as on sales, so if the PEP manager sells £500 of ICI shares and puts the money into BP there will be brokers' commissions on about £1,000 of dealings plus the stamp duty on the purchase. How much dealing costs add up to during a year depends on the frequency with which the shares are swapped around; with a dis-cretionary PEP that depends on the PEP manager, with a non-discretionary plan it depends on the investor. Unless a PEP invests only in unit trusts, however, there will be at least one set of dealing costs in most cases on the investment as it is initially put into shares.

Some managers will send details of transactions made on

a PEP holders' behalf as soon as they are made; others inform investors only with their annual statement from the managers.

Other charges

The government introduced PEPs with the intention of investors becoming more involved in individual companies than they are with shares owned at one stage removed through vehicles such as unit trusts or investment trusts. That means the investor being able to attend the annual shareholders' meetings of the companies in which he or she holds shares, being able to vote either at those meetings or by proxy, and receiving information sent by companies to their shareholders. The government has thus ruled that PEP-holders must be permitted by plan managers to exercise those rights – unfortunately the government has also allowed managers to make a charge to shareholders demanding their rights.

The annual report and accounts of a company must be sent to PEP-holders, however, as must the accounts of a unit trust. These accounts, typically glossy booklets from the main companies, contain statutory information such as the profit and loss account showing how the company performed over its accounting year (though these figures have usually been released to the Stock Exchange and been reported in newspapers several weeks previously) plus a balance sheet showing its assets and debts and a statement showing where the firm raised its finance over the year and how it spent it. There will also be a list of the directors and the shares in the company which they own, plus the notice of the annual shareholders' meeting at which some of those directors will be re-elected if investors approve. A statement from the company's auditors will indicate whether the company's account are a true and fair reflection of affairs, or if not, why not.

The accounts are usually accompanied by a statement from the chairman too, which explains why the company has performed well or badly over the past period and what plans the company may have for the future. Often there are pictures of the company's activities. A number of companies' accounts also include coupons entitling holders to discounts on certain of the firm's products or services. All that, including such perks, should be available to PEP investors.

In many cases, having details of the annual meeting's time and location from the company's report and accounts will be sufficient to allow PEP-holders to go to it and attend if they wish, though names are more frequently checked against shareholders' registers nowadays because of security considerations and checks are often made at potentially controversial meetings in an attempt to exclude hecklers. Entry to meetings may be interesting (though most company meetings are deadly dull) and entitle the PEP investor to share in the drinks or snacks frequently given to investors afterwards, but it does not entitle the PEP investor to participate in the meeting.

A company chairman can allow questions to be asked only by shareholders able to prove their validity and voting is restricted to such people. For the PEP investor to claim those rights he will require the agreement of the PEP manager who holds his share certificates and in whose name the shares will be registered. It is for allowing that right to be taken up that some PEP managers make a charge.

The TSB Group, for instance, demands £10 for meetings attended; Gartmore charges £40, BAT £75 and the FS investment management group £120. Many of the smaller PEP managers, particularly stockbrokers and accountants, make no charge at all.

Quoted companies send their shareholders communications other than the annual report and accounts during the course of the year, most notably a short interim statement of their profits and trading in the first six months of their accounting year. This too often appears in the press, either as an article or as an advertisement, so PEP-holders are not deprived of the content even if they do not elect to receive the company's version. Other communications from companies can be more important; they may be offering new shares to existing shareholders at below the current market level, they may be holding an extra-ordinary general meeting besides the annual meeting at which they are seeking special permission to issue shares or make a takeover or even to sack directors. The company may be subject of a takeover bid with the bidder posting out circulars detailing its offer and reasons for acceptance while the company itself argues for or against the bid. PEP managers must be prepared to allow their investors to see such information or exercise such additional rights, but they can charge extra.

Normally it would be argued that investors should be responsible by demanding and valuing such rights. The price put on them by many PEP managers means that investors have to question their value – and in most cases the answer is to do without. The vast majority of shareholders who do have these rights do not exercise them on most issues. Company meetings are at the wrong time of day or in the wrong part of the country for most shareholders and their content is usually uncontroversial.

A PEP holder feeling strongly about an issue will probably find that there are other people prepared to make similar views known who are able to speak and vote more easily. Any particular PEP investor's small holding is unlikely to sway a vote at a large company even if there is a controversial issue, and votes are not wasted – PEP managers can use their investors' holdings to vote as they see fit. Similarly the PEP managers will look after their investors' interests by doing what they think is right if they receive a bid from another company for shares or if new shares are offered. Giving up investors' rights is not a good thing, but it becomes a good thing at some of the prices demanded.

In conclusion, charges should be watched closely, but managers with high charges for one particular part of their service can be cheap on another, and high charges for services that will rarely be used need not be of great concern. Though charges are guaranteed and performance is not, it is the latter which matters.

9 UNCOMPLICATING SHARES

Whatever sort of PEP you choose, the money will ultimately go into shares. It may stay in cash for a time, but it has to be invested in shares or unit trusts to qualify for the tax benefits. If it goes into units, the units are invested in shares. What those shares are or their characteristics need not necessarily concern the unit investor, nor particularly the person investing in a PEP through a discretionary plan whose manager makes all the decisions. But any PEP investor who holds shares directly, including investment trust shares, may soon find himself involved with such matters as rights issues, dividends or even bids, and the details of these that appear on the manager's regular statements. This chapter is intended to give a very brief guide to some of the aspects of shares which the PEP investor may encounter.

What exactly is a share?

If someone started a business and owned all of it he could simply own the assets of that business and collect the profits. Alternatively, the business could be owned by a company and the company could be owned by the business person. If that person wanted to give half the business to a colleague, however, it would be necessary to make the business into an entity in its own right. This could mean forming a partnership or a company: if at least two shares in the company are created, each person can own one share each. Some small businesses have just two shares, and many just 100. As stakes in a family business are given to relatives and split between children, or as outsiders are brought in, it soon becomes necessary to have more than just a few dozen shares, however. A prospering business with few shares would mean that each share was worth a very large sum – possibly more than the share's owner wants to give away or sell at one time. Even private businesses are frequently split into thousands of shares therefore; by the time a company goes public on the Stock Exchange there are usually millions. Marks & Spencer, for instance, has well over 2,500 million shares, each representing an equal part of the business, and each with equal voting rights. There are only about 270,000 shareholders in Marks & Spencer though, most of them owning fewer than 2,000 shares.

Certificates

The shares are represented by certificates, not one for each share, but effectively one for each shareholding. Most public companies' certificates are now dull pieces of paper with computer text on them, not highly-decorated engraved certificates. They bear the name of the company and the name of the holder and the number of shares which the certificate represents. Although the pieces of paper are not to be treated carelessly, they only represent ownership, the certificates are not proof of ownership themselves for most purposes. If one is lost or destroyed, they can (at a small cost in many instances) be replaced; any investor's ownership of shares is registered with the company. The exception is newly issued shares in some companies, which are not registered immediately. Many of the privatisation issues were made on that basis – successful applicants were sent an allotment letter telling them how many shares they had, and that letter constituted proof of ownership. It was not until second tranches of the subscription price were paid on these shares that their owners' names were entered onto the share register. There are 'bearer shares' whose certificate does constitute proof, but these are rare. Nevertheless, many stockbrokers will ask to have the certificate before accepting a sell instruction, particularly from a new client.

Share prices

All shares have a nominal value, usually of 25p, but they can be £1, 1p or virtually any other value. That is usually the sum of money which was originally subscribed when the company first created its shares; the nominal value has virtually no relevance to shareholders later, however.

The price of a share is determined by the price that investors are prepared to pay. If a share is in demand its price will rise; if investors are reluctant to buy, prices would fall. What determines that demand will be the prospects for the company or the belief that the shares will be in demand by other investors later. Stock Exchange market-makers act as wholesalers and quote prices at which they will buy or sell a particular share. If they were selling too cheaply they would be swamped by demand from investors' stockbrokers and would not be able to buy enough stock; if they try selling too expensively they will find few buyers. Prices thus find their level. There are in fact two prices: an offer price at which investors can buy, and a slightly lower bid price at which they sell. The difference covers the market makers' costs.

Dividends

Companies usually pay out part of their profits to their shareholders as dividends, and if a company is doing well it can afford a larger dividend. It is possible to continue paying dividends even when a company makes a trading loss, by dipping into reserves built up in past years, but there are limits to how long that can continue. Not only may the company not have the cash to make payments if it is trading at a loss, it is legally prohibited from making payments if all the past accumulated profits have been distributed. All other things being equal, the more dividend that investors receive, the more attractive a share is and thus the more they will pay for it. If investors believe that a company will do well in the future and will thus be able to pay good returns in the future, they will be prepared to buy cheaply now. The trick is to anticipate the profits improvement before other investors, but each item of news that could affect future profits can affect investors' demand and thus the share price. Prospects of an interest rate rise would thus knock the share price of a highly borrowed company; a fall in the price of oil would hit an oil company's price but could help the shares of a company consuming considerable quantities of oil; or news of a new order could help a firm. Remember, though, that opening one new branch will make no great impact on the profits of a group the size of Sainsbury or Marks & Spencer, and that the company benefiting from the fall in oil prices may find its imported material prices rise because of the fall in the pound's international value caused by the oil price cut. Forecasting is not easy.

Most large companies pay two dividends a year. The size of the payment is announced on the day that the company reveals its half-yearly trading performance and profits, and its full-year's results. Payment is usually made to investors who are on the register at that date or a date up to a month or so later. The actual dividend may not then be paid until another month or so has elapsed. The final dividend cannot be paid until after the company has held its annual meeting and shareholders have approved payment: that meeting requires notice to be given, usually when the annual accounts are dispatched, but that is not until some weeks after release of the year's results in most cases.

Most shareholders would receive a cheque for the value of their dividend (after deduction of income tax at the basic rate by the company) or have it paid straight into a bank account; PEP investors' dividends must be paid into the PEP and the plan manager will recoup the tax already deducted. That could take a further month for the tax element to be repaid by the Inland Revenue.

Clearly anyone buying shares just before the date when registered investors will be sent a dividend has a better deal than those buying just after that date. The share price thus reflects that advantage. If the dividend was 3p, the share price would be about 3p higher before the date used to determine dividend payments than afterwards, all other things being equal. Shares still with the entitlement to a dividend are referred to as being 'cum-dividend', then become 'ex-dividend' afterwards. Newspapers mark shares 'x–d' in their price lists when the shares have become ex-dividend to explain the price movement and to tell investors what they are getting.

Yields

The relationship between a share price and the dividend paid is called the yield. This is a percentage, like a rate of interest, so a 100p share paying 3p dividend has a 3 per cent yield. Dividends differ from interest rates though, not only because they can fall or disappear entirely, but also because they are paid only to people holding them on specific dates. A share held for four months between dividend dates would give the investor no income at all, whereas money in a bank account for four months would receive a third of a year's interest. And even though a dividend may stay the same year after year, the yield can alter constantly. When the share price is 100p the 3p dividend gives it a 3 per cent yield. If the shares fell in price to 90p the 3p dividend gives a 3.3 per cent yield at that price. The person who bought at 100p does not benefit from the rise in the yield though – indeed, the investor has lost because of the share price fall.

Yields tend to be lower than interest rates. A typical recent return is little over 3 per cent. That is acceptable to investors because they are confident that the actual dividend payment will rise over the years as the company makes greater profits. If the company paying 3p can increase its payment at the rate of 20 per cent a year it will be giving investors 3.6p next year, 4.32p the year after, 5.18p after that, and so on. In seven years the company would be paying more than 10p which is over 10 per cent on the original 100p investment; in 11 years the return would be over 22 per cent. Investors are prepared to accept low returns now for high returns later. If investors insisted on receiving 10 per cent now they would offer only 30p for the shares of the company paying 3p dividends; it is investors who determine the share price depending on what yield they seek, therefore.

But if future investors are also prepared to accept a 3 per cent yield now because of anticipated growth, they will be prepared to pay 120p for the shares in the year when the company gives a 3.6p dividend. The investor thus sees the capital value of his shares grow as well as receiving increasing dividends. When the shares are paying a dividend of 10p, investors would offer about 350p for the shares to secure a 3 per cent yield.

If it looks like the company will not be able to sustain its rate of dividend growth, however – possibly because of a downturn in the economy or a downturn in that company's particular business – investors will demand a higher yield initially so that they reach the adequate dividend levels sooner. If the profits outlook is bad, therefore, the market could expect shares to yield 4 per cent. That would mean the company paying 3p sees its shares fall to 75p to give that 4 per cent yield to a buyer. Share prices have thus fallen because the outlook has deteriorated.

A company paying no dividend at all clearly gives its investors no yield. That does not mean that the shares are worthless though; investors look to the future and may be able to see prospects of a dividend eventually being made. The price they offer for shares will reflect the wait they have for their payment, though they may sell to another anticipating investor before the payment is ever actually made.

Price-earnings ratios

A company's earnings are the sum it has left from pre-tax profits after paying tax and dividend to preference shareholders, who are entitled to their fixed payment first. Interest, wages and the cost of premises and materials used are allowed for before the pre-tax profit figure is calculated. A few other small items also affect the earnings calculation but need not concern readers. These earnings, divided by the number of shares that the company has issued, give an 'earnings per share' figure which is effectively the after tax profit per share, or how much money the company made in a year that it could give to shareholders.

Some investors like to compare the earnings per share figure with the share price to produce a price-earnings ratio or PE ratio. If a company has earnings of 5p a share and a 100p share price it has a PE of 20. Some newspapers quote the PE ratio alongside the share prices they quote, and the current yield figure as well. The PE ratio is a way of reducing all companies to a comparable basis.

A large brewery making £100 million a year profits might have the same PE ratio as a small brewery making only £1 million. The ratio shows how many years, at current profit rates, it would take a company to produce sufficient earnings to equal the share price. If one company has a lower price-earnings ratio than another the first is either underrated or the market believes that its prospects for increasing profits are less good than the second. Low PE ratios are one way of spotting shares which are underpriced relative to their earnings – though some companies remain 'underpriced' for long periods.

Dividend cover

Companies do not pay out all of their dividends or earnings. They need to retain some of their cash for investment and they like to leave some of their profits in reserves to strengthen their accounts. A company paying out only a small part of its profits as dividend can afford to take quite a knock on its profits and still maintain the payment, however, while a company already paying out the whole of its profits can only keep up its previous dividend level by dipping into past reserves – which weakens the accounts and the company's backing.

The relationship between how much a company could pay in dividend from the year's profits and how much it does pay is the dividend cover. If a company with earnings

PERSONAL EQUITY PLANS

of 5p pays 3p dividend, the payment is covered 1.67 times.
A cover of less than 1 means that a company is dipping into
reserves: covers of 2 are typical and a cover of say, 10,
suggests that the business could afford to be much more
generous in its payment. Perhaps it will be.

Net asset value

There are other yardsticks applied to shares. Some
companies are measured by their assets rather than their
capacity to earn – investment trusts and property companies, for instance. If a property company with £100
million of buildings and no debt were put into liquidation
then there ought to be £100 million to distribute between
shareholders (unless the taxmen take a slice) and the value
of all the shares should total that £100 million. If the
company had 100 million shares, they would each have
asset backing of £1 each, or if an investment trust with £100
million of other companies' shares were wound-up there
should be £100 million to distribute to shareholders and
that should be the value of their total shareholdings. In fact
the £100m or the £1 per share is the shares' asset value and
prices offered for the shares can be different. Traditionally,
both property companies' and investment trusts' shares
have traded at less than the shares' asset value. This
discount reflects both the problems of winding up a
company and the tax that would have to be paid on assets
sold, plus a market reluctance to pay full price. In 1987,
however, before the crash, most property companies found
that their share prices rose above the asset value of the
shares. This partly reflected rises in the property market
since the asset value was last calculated, but also an
anticipation of future growth.

Because many companies have borrowings – modest
usually in investment trusts but often quite significant in
property firms – the debt has to be allowed for in
calculating net asset values. The company with £100 million
of buildings but £40 million of debt has net assets of only
£60 million – or 60p a share if there are 100 million shares in

issue. The share price would probably be between 50p and just over 60p, therefore.

Rights issues and clawbacks

When a company is formed, the original investors sub-scribe money which the company can use for trading. The shares given to those original investors can be sold and resold at ever-increasing prices as the company prospers, but the company itself receives none of the advantage of the rise in its share price. It may need more capital as it grows though, so the company may choose to issue new shares. Unofficial rules imposed on companies dictate that any issue increasing its share capital by more than a small amount must be offered first to the existing shareholders. This is because the shareholders own the business and if new investors were to be allowed in on any preferential terms, it would be to the detriment of the existing holders.

Companies also realise that if they need more capital, then it may be easiest to raise it from those people who have already chosen to invest in the company. They therefore offer the new shares to the existing investors, and they offer them exactly in relation to investors' current holdings – larger shareholders being offered more than small ones.

If a company was to double its number of shares it would offer one new share for each existing one. This is called a 1-for-1 rights issue – it being every shareholder's right to take them up. Shareholders are under no obligation to accept the rights shares, however.

Normally rights issue shares are offered at a small discount to the market price to encourage shareholders to take them up. A share with a 100p market price before a rights issue was announced might offer new shares at 90p – but it could offer them at, say, 50p. National Westminster Bank is one company that has made such 'deep-discount' rights issues in recent years. But once the rights issue is announced, the market price of the shares will adjust to reflect the offer of cheap shares; the person with one 100p share who can buy another 90p share effectively has two shares worth a combined 190p, making both worth 95p each. That is the level that the market price will adjust to. So if the investor's 100p share is going to fall in value to 95p he may as well subscribe for the 90p share he is entitled to. If he does not have the necessary cash, the investor can either borrow to buy the shares, then sell it at the anticipated profit and repay his debt, or he can sell the 'right' to the new share to someone who can afford it, while the investor holds onto his original share. The right would be sold for around the 5p difference between the subscription cost of the new share and its expected market value when trading in the new shares starts.

Because PEPs cannot borrow and because they may have their funds fully invested in shares, PEP managers may face this problem when companies in which they have invested make rights issues. PEP managers may have sufficient cash anyway, or they could sell a different share to obtain the money to subscribe for the rights, or they could sell the rights and retain only the original shares, putting the proceeds of the rights sale back into the PEP. They could also sell the rights on sufficient of their holding to provide the cash to subscribe on the rest.

Rights shares are not really cheap shares because they reduce the value of the existing holding. Someone owning one per cent of a company who took up his rights in an issue would still hold one per cent afterwards – though it would be one per cent of a larger company; larger to the extent of all the new money subscribed in the issue. Shareholders do often lose if they ignore shares offered to them in rights issues, though.

If the stock market falls in the weeks between an issue being announced and shareholders having to pay for the new shares, investors may choose not to accept them. If a company whose shares are at 100p offers new shares at 90p but then sees its market price fall to 85p, it would be silly to subscribe at 90p. The company nevertheless receives its money; it underwrites the issue by paying a group of City institutions a small fee to agree to take any shares that existing investors reject.

One further complication for PEPs investors is that rights

issues do not always involve the issue of new ordinary shares. Instead, existing holders of ordinary shares (as PEP investors would be) could be offered convertible loan stock, debentures or preference shares, none of which can be held in a PEP. In such instances, the PEP manager's choice is to ignore the rights – however valuable they might be, to sell the rights if there is a market for them (but unlike offers of new ordinary shares, there may not yet be an existing market for a new class of preference shares) or to offer them directly to the PEP investor to take up outside the personal equity plan.

There is a further complication, too. Changes in the rules on when shares should be offered to a company's existing investors mean that shareholders are increasingly frequently being offered new shares in their company, but under 'clawback provisions' rather than as rights. In most other respects, these clawbacks are the same as a rights issue; the right to take up clawback shares cannot be sold, however.

With a rights issue a company decides that it requires cash, possibly to finance an acquisition, and raises it by offering new shares to existing investors at a discount to the current market price. In case investors do not want the new shares, underwriters agree to buy any not taken up. If the company instead decided to issue new shares directly to the people from whom it was making the acquisition, then those shares have under the clawback provisions to be offered to existing investors. Again, they would usually be offered at a discount, and if existing investors did not buy them, they would be taken up by the people selling the business to the company – or if they intended selling the shares immediately for cash, by the same sort of underwriters. These deals are called a vendor placing. The shares are placed with or by the vendor of whatever the other company is acquiring. But because the rights to receiving the shares cannot be sold without also selling the original shares themselves, investors' only alternatives are to ignore the offer of new shares, to sell the whole shareholding, to find the cash to take up the new shares or sell sufficient of the existing holding to provide the finance to subscribe for the new shares on the remainder of the holding. For a PEP manager, subscribing for the rights on the whole shareholding can be done only if there is sufficient cash inside the PEP or by selling one of the other shares held by the PEP.

Scrip issues

Rights issues give the investor the chance of subscribing for new shares at an apparently cheap price – though because the price of the existing shares will fall to average out the cheapness of the new shares offered, the investor does not really gain by buying the new shares, he or she merely loses if they fail to buy them. Scrip issues are new shares given away by the company free, but again the mathematics of the exercise mean that there is no real gain. Scrip issues are also known as bonus or capitalisation issues. If a company's shares trade on the stockmarket at £10 and the company makes a 1-for-1 scrip issue – that is, it gives away one new share for each one currently held – the investor will have two shares. But because the company is not worth any more than it was, the shares are worth only £5 each, so the value of the shareholding is unchanged. Shareholders looking at the price of their shares in the newspapers should watch for a notation such as 'ex-scrip' or 'ex-cap' (meaning ex-capitalisation issue) applying to a share. Suddenly seeing that a share price has halved or even fallen to a quarter of its previous value can provide a nasty shock when all it really means is that a scrip issue has given investors more shares.

Companies do it when their share price become unwieldy. Buying £20 shares is difficult for the small investor wanting to put in, say, £250 – he is liable to find his actual investment is anything up to £20 below what he expected because of the small number of shares that the sum buys; had the shares been divided into 10 shares with a value of about £2, the stockbroker can always buy a number of shares taking the value of the investment very close to that which the client wanted to invest. American and Japanese companies tend to have very high value shares; British companies prefer to have their's priced at about £5 or so.

But there can be genuine advantages from a scrip issue. Because the larger number of lower priced shares makes the company's shares more marketable, the shares may be in greater demand by investors. Rather than the £10 share turning into two £5 shares therefore, it may become two shares, of say £5.05.

Secondly, while a company which has seen its share price soar from £1 or so to £20 may be keen to bring the price back to a manageable level of £2, it would not do so if it thought that the price might then collapse back to 30p or so because of poor trading; better to do nothing and allow it to collapse to a healthier looking £3. Making a scrip issue shows some confidence by the management, though plenty of managers have misplaced confidence. Thirdly, while companies doubling the number of shares in issue should cut their dividend per share by half to leave investors with the same income, they often do not make such a drastic cut – or might even make no cut at all. The shareholders' income can rise, therefore. The same real increase usually applies to rights issues too: the dividend on the new, cheap, shares is usually at least the same as was paid on the existing shares, so even though the price of the existing shares and the cheap shares average out, the dividends do not and the investor's return rises.

Takeovers

Much of the financial news in any newspaper concerns takeovers of one company by another, or battles to prevent a bid succeeding. Except in a few unusual cases, any company, quoted or not, is free to make an offer for any other, whether or not the company wants to be taken over. Over the past few years, a PEP investor would have been unlucky not to have been on one end or another of a takeover.

While the directors of the company being bid for will give their views on the offer, the success or failure of a bid lies solely with the shareholders – including people owning shares through PEPs. In many cases takeovers are agreed between the two companies, the directors of the one being bid for will recommend the offer and shareholders accept.

The terms that they have been offered will usually be either cash, shares in the company making the bid, or a choice between the two. It is up to the bidder, however, if he wants to offer only shares or only cash.

In many cases bids are not that simple at all. In some cases the directors of the company being bid for may not want to be taken over and will appeal to shareholders to protect the company's freedom – in 1987, for instance, Pilkington, the glass-makers, successfully fought a vigorous campaign to avoid being taken over by BTR. Sometimes the campaign does not succeed. Debenhams directors did not want their department stores company taken over by the Burton Group, but they lost. Or a company may face two different bids from different predators at the same time. The Distillers Company in 1986, for instance, faced simultaneous takeover offers from James Gulliver's Argyll Group (which it opposed) and from Guinness (which it supported). In the now notorious result, Guinness won. At the same time however, Imperial Group, the tobacco, beer and food company, faced simultaneous offers from United Biscuits and Hanson Trust. Imperial's directors supported United Biscuits and opposed Hanson – the shareholders chose Lord Hanson, however. The power lies with the investor.

During contentious bids such as those for Distillers or Pilkington or Imperial, shareholders are likely to find themselves bombarded with circulars and arguments. Newspapers tend to carry advertisements from the different sides arguing the merits of their cases too. Luckily, newspapers and stockbrokers will usually give independent advice on what action to take. And often it will be clear even to the disinterested investor what the best action is; if one company offers 110p cash and another 120p it is obvious which is best – though not obvious whether it would be better to accept neither and to retain the shares.

Small shareholders should not usually act quickly in bids. Often a takeover offer from one company will encourage another bidder to intervene. Obviously the second bidder must offer better terms than the first: that might provoke the first bidder into producing still better terms, which might make the second bidder go higher still. It does not always require two competing bidders to force up terms; if either directors or shareholders decline to accept the original terms the bidder will be forced to improve them or lose. Sometimes directors who have rejected an initial offer will give their support if the offer price is improved. If shareholders do accept an offer and the terms are then raised, the new terms must apply to those who have already accepted though: there is no penalty in being premature.

Bids usually take several weeks between terms being announced and victory or defeat being conceded and it is not until after victory is won that shareholders receive their cash or shares in the bidding company. Often a bidder will insist on achieving not 51 per cent of a company before declaring its bid 'unconditional' (that is, the point at which the bidder cannot back out) but on receiving support from holders of 90 per cent of shares. After a bidder has secured 90 per cent support it can use legal procedures to purchase the remaining shares compulsorily. If it achieves a lower figure it could have voting control through a majority share-holding, but the company could remain quoted with several thousands of outside shareholders holding the remaining shares. Those outside shareholders thus share in any future growth produced by the new parent company, but there are dangers in being locked into a minority of a company controlled by one shareholder. It is usually a situation to avoid.

Takeover bids are almost inevitably at above the previous market price of their target company and often at sub-stantially above. Shareholders wanting to take their profits do not necessarily need to wait for the bid to be finalised, however. Once a bid is made the market price of the com-pany will usually jump to reflect the offer, and the investor can sell through the stockmarket and take the profit.

That means paying stockbrokers' commission, however, and it means that if a better bid does emerge, the investor will not benefit from it because he no longer owns the shares. There are times when it is best to sell though. If a share trades at about 100p and a bidder offers 140p the market price of the share could jump to 150p because investors believe that this or another bidder will be forced to go higher or it might rise only to 130p or so because investors are not convinced that the offer will succeed. And if the bid fails, the market price is likely to fall back to little better than the original 100p. A shareholder might well prefer to obtain 150p from the market now in the belief that no better bid would emerge.

He or she might prefer to accept even 137p now, rather than wait several weeks for 140p. Or investors might be happy with 130p now because they think the company will fail to receive sufficient support for the offer from other shareholders or because the bid might be referred to the Monopolies & Mergers Commission, preventing it from proceeding at least until the Secretary of State for Trade had given it his approval (usually after a delay of more than six months). Bids are often withdrawn altogether if referred to the Monopolies Commission.

There are occasions when the shares of a company which has successfully fought off a bidder do not fall back again to well below the offer price. Sometimes the market will believe that another bidder may emerge; sometimes the company has argued its own case sufficiently well that the market re-rates the shares.

Frequently a company under attack will promise a large dividend rise as an inducement to existing investors to support it, and the prospect of that improved yield can be sufficient to support the share price. Fighting an unwanted takeover attempt concentrates managers' minds too. Once they are under attack they may start running the company better than they did, even to the point of restructuring the business or selling parts. That can leave shareholders with a better business. And directors are under a strong obligation to meet the often ambitious forecasts of profits which they tend to make during bids.

But if the investor wants to profit and does not want to sell in the market, he or she may still have a choice between accepting cash or accepting shares in the new company. Occasionally there is a third alternative of 'loan notes', a usually unquoted entitlement to receive a fixed dividend on a security which will be repaid by the bidding company at some specified future date.

Companies offer their own shares both because they do not have the cash to bid with, but also because some investors prefer 'paper' to cash. The investor accepting cash has effectively sold his shares, and that triggers a potential capital gains tax liability. If shares are accepted through a swap – say, two shares in the bidding company for each share currently held in the target company – there is no gains tax liability until the bidder's shares are eventually disposed of. Accepting shares in the bidder also allows the investor to retain an interest in the business he or she chose originally to invest in, even if that business will now be mixed in with the bidder's own activities. Or accepting shares in the bidder is a way of investing in that company without paying stamp duty or stockbrokers' charges or suffering the spread between the bid price of the target company and the offer price of the bidder.

But whereas the cash value of an offer is constant from day to day unless it is specifically increased, the value of a share swap will vary in line with the value of the bidder's shares in the market, and that might be affected by the bidder's prospects of winning the offer. While a bid usually lifts the share price of the target company, it often knocks that of the bidding company because of fears that the bidder is taking over a firm less good than itself or may have to stretch itself financially to do so. It is because the value of a share-swap can vary that investors should not make up their minds about a bid too early. If a company bid 140p a share cash for a rival and offered two of its own shares which are currently worth 70p, the 140p value of the paper terms would be identical. However, a strong rise in the stock market or of that company's share in particular could mean that several weeks later the 'paper' offer is worth 160p or so while the cash alternative is still 140p.

But if there was a fall in stock markets the target company's shares might not move. The paper terms might be worth 120p, but the now attractive 140p cash is still available.

The relative share prices are not the only points to watch,

however. The investor should consider the dividends of the company making the bid and the quality of its business if its shares are to be accepted. The company being bid for might have been paying 8p a share dividend. The bidder might pay only 2p, so even a two-for-one share swap would leave the investor's income halved. That is important for investors using a personal equity plan as a way of receiving income from shares tax-free.

With a PEP managed on a discretionary basis it will be the plan manager who decides what action to take during a bid. Whether or not the circulars dispatched by the two or more companies involved are passed onto the investor is the manager's decision – though in most cases they will not be. Non-discretionary PEP investors will have to make their own decisions. However, because there is no capital gains tax payable on PEP investments, the argument against accepting cash terms in case they trigger a tax liability can be ignored. Loan note alternatives can be ignored too because PEPs cannot hold these notes, which are merely a device for giving accepting shareholders what is almost cash but which defers any tax liability. If there is a choice, PEP investors can decide whether to accept a bidder's shares or cash, purely on the merits of whether the bidding company is a good one to include in the PEP portfolio, or whether the cash could be put to better use elsewhere.

Inside information

Companies often make moves which affect their share prices, or the prices of other companies' shares, substantially. So that all investors are treated equally, information about such moves is announced through the Stock Exchange, in theory at least, making it available to all investors simultaneously. Inevitably a number of people have to know about such moves before they are announced, however – the directors, their advisers and certain key members of staff, for instance. Such people may be tempted to buy or sell shares in anticipation of the expected movement in a company's shares or they may give the information to other people. This constitutes inside information, however, and it is now a criminal offence to deal on the basis of it. People finding themselves party to such information should resist the temptation to involve themselves in insider dealing. When a price does move sharply before a price-sensitive announcement the Stock Exchange authorities usually start an inquiry which requires brokers to give details of all deals they made in the shares at the time. An employee privy to inside information who might have bought even just 500 shares, or a relative to whom they mentioned that something was happening, would thus very likely find themselves exposed, even though their purchase or sale was not large enough to move the price.

There are grey areas as to what would constitute insider dealing. Buying Sainsbury shares after observing on a Saturday that a store has increased its number of customers would not be illegal. Observing that a local building company is involved in a lot of orders would not be either. Being told by a council official that the town's engineering company has submitted a planning application to turn its warehouse into a shopping centre might not be inside information once the application was on the public register. Being told by the official that talks were in progress with the engineering company about the possibility of submitting an application almost certainly would be. If in doubt, be careful. But having inside information is not a route to instant profit anyway. It is necessary to analyse whether it will be accepted favourably by the rest of the stock market when known, or disfavourably. Sometimes a company's shares rise when it announces a takeover because of the enhanced prospects for the combined firm; sometimes the shares fall because of the price that the bidder will have to pay and the damage that its earnings per share could suffer. Knowing about the bid in advance is not the same as anticipating the market reaction.

Stock Exchange settlement

The Stock Exchange divides up the year into a series of 'accounts' – most of them periods of a fortnight, though a few last three weeks, usually including bank holidays. With the exception of shares which are still dealt-in in allotment letter form because they have not been registered – and this includes the privatisation issues in most instances, until at least the second tranche the subscription price is paid – payment for shares bought or sold is not immediate. All the dealings done in each account period are taken together and 'settled' at the same time on 'account day' or 'settlement day', which is usually the second Monday after the account ends.

So for the account beginning on August 1, 1988, all dealings through until Friday, August 12 would be in that account. The dealings have to be settled on Monday, August 22. Shares bought on Wednesday, August 3 and sold profitably on the following Wednesday would not have to be paid for, therefore. The broker would not have asked for the purchase price until August 22 and he would also be sending the investor the proceeds of his subsequent deal on that date. The broker thus deducts the cost (including his commission) from the sale proceeds and sends the investor a cheque for the difference. The usual 0.5 per cent stamp duty is even waived for such deals within the account. Such rapid buying and selling is for speculators only, however – or people who realise their mistakes quickly. For the move to be made profitably, the investor must be sure that the price of the chosen stock will rise sufficiently within the account to cover the difference between the bid and offer price as well as the broker's charges. If the investor is wrong, he or she will have to send the broker a cheque on account day. If, as is more likely, the investor is selling one share during an account and buying another immediately or shortly afterwards, the sale proceeds of the one deal will coincide with the demand for payment on the purchase, and the broker will offset the two at account day. This means that it is theoretically possible to make a purchase early in the account and not sell the shares which will pay for that purchase until later in the same account; the PEP investor could thus have bought a second £2,400 of shares before selling the first £2,400 worth therefore (or whatever value the shares in the PEP had risen to), so effectively exceeding the limit temporarily.

A contract note should be sent by the broker as soon as the order to buy or sell is given by the investor. A share certificate is issued by the company itself or its registrars at some later date, though in most cases this will be retained by the PEP manager rather than by the investor.

Because the proceeds of sales are offset with the cost of purchases in the same account, there is less prospect of cash in the PEP exceeding the defined limits. Major transactions can be deducted with very little cash being required or being repaid, therefore.

10 HOW DO PEPS COMPARE WITH OTHER INVESTMENTS?

The words 'tax-free' have an appeal to people who think themselves highly taxed. The opportunity of getting something back from the taxman or the government has more than the simple financial attraction. But while those words are attached firmly to personal equity plans, potential investors should not forget that PEPs are only one of many investments which have limited tax advantages. For any particular investor a PEP may not be the best – though it may still be worthwhile taking one out. Below are some of the other investments with tax advantages, for comparison with PEPs.

Houses

A person's main home is a tax-free investment. The rise in value is not taxed as capital gain. True, the £2,400 maximum which can be put into a PEP will not buy a large house, but it would pay the complete interest on a £30,000 mortgage for a basic-rate income tax payer claiming that other tax perk of housing, mortgage interest relief. Anyway, the investor may be putting only £2,400 into a PEP because that is all that is permitted in a year; he or she may have a larger sum available for a larger mortgage, giving them a larger home. Or £2,400 may buy them a part of a home, say a new central heating system or patio for the property which they already own, but which will appreciate in value that much more with the improvement.

Life assurance

A life assurance policy taken out before the March 1984 budget still attracts tax relief on the premiums paid. For every £85 that the policyholder pays, the Inland Revenue still tops that up with £15, so that £100 of shares, or gilts, or property, or whatever is bought by the life company. There are tax advantages too, once that £100 is invested by the life company, which also apply to policies taken out after that budget day, but policyholders paying an £85 premium on those policies buy only £85 of assets. It is impossible now to start a policy which benefits from this generous tax relief, but it is quite legitimate to continue a pre-1984 policy for as long as possible. And in case you think that you have never bought life assurance, remember that that is exactly what the endowment policy is which is probably being used to repay your mortgage. (Most housebuyers in recent years have been sold an endowment policy as a means of repaying the loan, largely because of the tax advantages.) Rather than stop paying premiums of a pre-1984 policy or rather than surrender it, it is better to continue the payments than to divert the cash into a PEP.

Pensions

There is no longer premium relief on life assurance policies (and it was at only half the income tax rate anyway) but it remains on contributions to pension policies or company pension schemes. Each £1 put into a pension is deducted from the contributor's pay before his income tax is worked out. For a basic rate taxpayer that means that each £1 going into a pension would have been worth only 73p in the shops; for a top rate taxpayer it would have been worth just 40p. And once that £1 goes into the pension fund it enjoys all the benefits that a PEP does – the dividends received from shares are received free of income tax, the capital gains from the rise in the shares' value are free of capital gains tax. And a pension fund is permitted to invest in a wider range of investments than a PEP: funds can buy shares in foreign-registered companies, unquoted companies, property, gilts and much more.

The snag is, however, that there can be an extremely long wait before the investment can be realised. It certainly cannot be turned into cash in a few days by most people. Secondly, only a certain proportion of income can be contributed to a pension scheme, 17½ per cent in most cases. The majority of people are nowhere near to reaching that limit, but however good pensions are, not everyone is free to pour in more cash.

Business expansion schemes

The Business Expansion Scheme, or BES, was an earlier wheeze from Chancellor Nigel Lawson. In some ways it is an opposite of the personal equity plan. The BES allows individuals to buy shares in certain companies and offset the cost against their pay, just like pension contributions, and just like the French *Loi Monory* Mr Lawson mentioned in his 1986 budget speech when introducing PEPs. In the short term at least this is a far more substantial saving: a person earning £25,000 could invest less than £20,000 in a BES company and eliminate his income tax liability totally for that year. A 50 per cent taxpayer investing £5,000 through the BES *saves* £5,000 tax by doing so, a top-rate taxpayer saves even more. The disadvantage is that no companies as sound as ICI or Marks & Spencer can be BES companies. Indeed, while PEP companies have to have their shares listed in the United Kingdom, BES companies must not have share quotations. They tend to be considerably riskier than the big quoted companies, therefore, and the government has increased that risk by specifically excluding farming, property and other asset-based investments.

Another snag is that the original income tax concession is lost if the shares are sold within five years, but the gains are now free of capital gains tax, putting them on a par with PEP companies. The £40,000 annual maximum that can be put into BES companies may be a limit for some, though not as limiting as £2,400 into PEPs.

115

Gilt-edged stock

The fixed-interest rate stock which the government issues periodically is now free of capital gains. The dividends are still taxed as income at the investor's marginal income tax rate, but all the movements in the price of the stocks are now tax-free, however long the stock has been held for. Price movements over a year can be as substantial as the rise in the FT Index if market interest rates are fluctuating, and although selling prices can fall too, the government will always eventually redeem the stocks at their full par value when they mature. Gilts, of course, are one of the investments which a PEP cannot buy.

National Savings

Besides gilts, the government offers tax advantages through National Savings. A number of the regular savings products are tax-free. Premium bond winnings, for instance, are untaxed, and are paid out at a level equal to 7 per cent of the whole amount of bonds bought. Over time, therefore, a sufficiently large bondholder's winnings ought to average that rate, but to a top-rate taxpayer, that rate is worth 17.5 per cent. The inflation-linked bonds are tax-free too, though with inflation so much lower than interest rates, there has been little attraction in such bonds in recent years. Better are the guaranteed return savings certificates such as the 33rd Issue which also promises to pay 7 per cent to investors holding them for five years, tax-free. Again, for a top rate taxpayer, that is the equivalent of receiving 17.5 per cent gross from an alternative savings medium. The Yearly Plan is a monthly account similar to the certificates with a maximum investment level identical to the PEPs' £200 monthly limit. Again, the return is guaranteed and tax-free. Withdrawing savings should have the cash in the investor's hands as soon as he would receive the proceeds from selling a PEP. The Yearly Plan and guaranteed-rate certificates do pay lower rates in early years and higher rates in later years, but their main snag for many people is simply the amount that can be invested in them: £2,400 maximum into the Yearly Plan, £1,000 into any one issue of the certificates, though often more than one issue is made per year, and sometimes the limit has been £10,000.

So there are plenty of tax-efficient alternatives to PEPs. In many cases, if an investor had just £500 to invest he or she might find a better or more flexible place for it than a PEP. However, there does not necessarily have to be a choice. Whenever the government is giving money away it imposes snags – if it did not the rush into the schemes might be overwhelming. One of the common snags is simply to limit the amount that can go into the scheme, hence the £2,400 limit on PEPs, the £40,000 BES limit, the 17.5 per cent pension ceiling, the £2,400 on Yearly Plan, the other National Savings certificates' £1,000 and the £30,000 limit on mortgages for interest relief. If the saver finds that he has reached a ceiling on one tax-efficient investment and still has money to invest, he is quite free to put his extra cash into another tax-efficient investment.

Personal equity plans do not have to be instead of other investments; they can both supplement them and complement them.

11 SOME QUESTIONS AND ANSWERS

I'm not a taxpayer. Should I have a PEP?
The advantage of PEPs is that investors pay no income tax or capital gains tax. If you for some reason are not a taxpayer and do not expect to become one, then there is no point investing through a PEP. You are probably better off with a unit trust.

Can I give a PEP to someone else?
You can give an amount of money to another person for them to invest in a PEP, but the recipient will have to sign a PEP form and declare that they have no other PEP for that year.

Can I sell my PEP intact?
No. The Inland Revenue does not regard a PEP as a separate item of property. The investor holds merely a series of shares or unit trusts. These can be sold but the buyer could not enjoy the past tax benefits of the investments and could only enjoy future tax benefits if they were bought through a new PEP properly registered in the buyer's name.

Is there an official PEP form?
No. Individual PEP managers will provide their own forms.

What if I start two PEPs in a year?
If one person starts two PEP plans in the same calendar year, then both will be declared invalid, and all normal taxes will have to be paid on the investments on both. Application forms require investors to declare that they

have not subscribed for another PEP in the same year. Prosecutions and penalties could follow, though the investor does have the usual appeal rights.

If I under-invest one year can I top up in the next?
No. Up to £2,400 can be put into a PEP in any calendar year. If less than that is invested one year, the next year's limit cannot be increased.

Will the £2,400 annual ceiling be raised?
The government did not say when PEPs were launched that the ceiling was fixed for ever. Most similar limits on investment or tax thresholds are reviewed and raised periodically, but not necessarily every year, and not necessarily in line with inflation.

What if I emigrate?
People who have started personal equity plans and who then cease being UK residents for tax purposes do not lose their tax advantages. No new money can be put into the PEP and no new PEPs can be started once they stop qualifying, but existing investments do not have to be withdrawn, and they will continue to roll up free of UK tax.

What if I die?
A PEP itself cannot be left to the beneficiaries of a will, but the actual shares in the plan, or their value, can be. Even if an investor dies before the end of the qualifying tax year the gains made up until then will remain tax-free: from the date of death any dividends received and any additional capital gains will be subject to tax, however, by whoever inherits them. Inheritance tax could be payable too if the value of the PEP means that the whole estate exceeds the threshold for this tax.

Do I need to know my National Insurance number?
Applicants for a PEP investor must give the manager their name and address, plus their National Insurance number and, if they know it, the name of their tax office. National Insurance numbers are demanded by the Inland Revenue

as the method of ensuring that no person has two PEPs. The number can be found on wage slips. Most plan managers will not demand to see proof of the number. Some people who have never worked in Britain, including some married women and expatriates who return as pensioners, will have had no number issued; they can buy a PEP by quoting a tax reference – a husband's reference for non-working married women – or pension number. Self-employed people usually pay Class II National Insurance contributions, so have a number. Those whose profits are less than £2,125 in the tax-year ending in 1988 will be able to produce a letter of exemption from the Department of Health & Social Security – which the PEP manager will want to see with a tax reference.

If prospective PEP investors cannot find their National Insurance number they can still start a plan if they can quote their tax reference number. The PEP manager can accept the application provisionally and add the National Insurance number later. That is useful for people who have left their applications until late December and who cannot locate their number.

What do I have to tell the taxman?
Nothing. If for any reason the Inland Revenue asked questions you are obliged to answer, but that is unlikely, and you need to declare nothing voluntarily.

What if tax rates change?
As PEP investors pay no tax, there will be no change. But if income tax rates fall there will be less advantage investing through a PEP. A basic-rate income taxpayer saves less by avoiding 25 per cent tax than by avoiding 27 per cent tax. Similarly, a fall in higher rates mean less saving, though the actual amount received by the PEP investor is the same whether income tax is zero or 100 per cent. The same applies to capital gains taxes too. If the rate is lowered or the threshold at which it is payable increases significantly, there will be less tax saved on profits.

120

Can I offset capital losses in my PEP against gains elsewhere?
No. Gains inside PEPs are free of capital gains tax, but if the shares produce a loss (or a loss after allowing for inflation) it cannot normally be applied to reduce gains made on other shares or assets realised. Investors buying high-risk shares in the hope of making a high reward should bear that in mind if the investment does become a loser instead. If an enormous loss had been made before the end of the qualifying year, however (which could be nearly two years after the investment was made originally if the money was invested at the start of a year) it might be worth deliberately terminating the PEP through a withdrawal or other breach of the rules. That would make the loss offsettable against other gains realised in the same tax year.

Although that would mean that the use of a PEP based on that original year was now forfeited, this might be little loss if the value of the investment has become so little that it could be transferred into only a small investment in any other shares – and if the company whose shares were bought has gone bust making the shares worthless, then exploiting the capital loss is all that is left for the PEP investor.

Can my PEP buy shares in my own company?
Yes. If your company is quoted and qualifies for inclusion in a PEP, the managers of a discretionary PEP may well choose to buy its shares, especially if it is a major firm. The PEP manager will not necessarily hold onto the shares long-term though. A non-discretionary PEP whose shares are chosen by the investor himself can specifically choose such a share, though, and retain it. Remember, though, that just because a firm is a good employer does not mean its shares will perform well. Bear in mind that putting your investment and your employment in the same company is concentrating your eggs into one basket. And do not use inside information.

I'm a director of a company whose shares my PEP owns. Must I declare them?
Technically, yes. A director would not normally know

immediately what shares a discretionary PEP manager was buying on his behalf, but if these did include shares in the director's own company, they would have to be declared in the usual manner.

Can I put my existing shares into my PEP?
Only by selling them completely and using the proceeds to repurchase shares through the PEP – and selling could produce a realised profit which leaves the seller with a capital gains tax liability. Many unit trust groups do normally accept shares in exchange for units: for PEPs they too would have to sell the shares or existing units and to re-invest the cash. Both unit groups and stockbrokers will in many cases perform 'bed-and-breakfast' deals in which shares or units are technically sold, then repurchased soon afterwards, usually the following day.

This is normally done for investors wanting to realise sufficient of their past capital gains to use up their annual exemption, or by investors wanting to crystallise their losses to offset against gains. The brokers or unit trust companies do this at a reduced cost, though stamp duty usually has to be paid by the investor on the repurchase. A similar bed-and-breakfast (so-called because the broker holds them overnight for the investor) arrangement can be performed for PEP investors if PEP managers are willing, but the investor must actually sell the shares or units so that cash can be given to the PEP manager to buy back the investments.

Why are PEP investment in unit trusts limited?
Originally Chancellor of the Exchequer Nigel Lawson wanted unit trusts and investment trusts excluded from PEPs altogether. He considers them too far removed from real share ownership – they do not allow investors to receive the accounts and other information of the companies held by the trust, and they do not allow investors to attend meetings. Given the costs of receiving those privileges with a PEP, investors are unlikely to take up their rights anyway. Mr Lawson did, grudgingly, eventually

allow investment in unit and investment trusts, but only within the strict limitations described on page 49.

What if the units become more than 25 per cent of the PEP?
Investment in unit trusts or investment trusts is limited to £420 in a year or a quarter of the year's total PEP investment if that is greater. It is irrelevant what happens to the value of those investments later, however. Even if three-quarters of the investment is put into shares which collapse in value while the one quarter in unit trusts soars – so giving the units far more than a quarter of the PEP's value – it does not matter. It is the proportion of the original investment each year which is important.

Can I apply for new share issues?
The British Petroleum share issue in the autumn of 1987 was the first which permitted PEPs to apply. It was argued that applications for previous issues were impossible because they did not guarantee that investors would receive shares, whereas everyone who registered their interest in the BP issue was promised at least a minimum number. PEP managers had to register interest on behalf of investors but were given no special preference over other investors. Of course, the BP offer proved a flop anyway.

Are multiple applications possible?
If a PEP manager applies for new shares through a plan in the manner described above, the individual could apply for new shares in his or her own right too. Normally that would constitute a multiple application which, with many of the privatisation issues at least, can be a criminal offence, or at the minimum could lead to one or both of the applications being declared invalid. With the British Petroleum PEP plan, the Treasury stated that as long as the investor was unaware that the PEP manager had also applied on the investor's behalf, then two legal and valid applications could be made. If the investor was aware that the PEP manager was applying for BP shares too, a second application would be a multiple application. Moral: don't ask.

Can I own fractions of shares?
No. But a PEP manager may buy fractions of unit trusts. A manager seeking to put £100 into £7 shares will have cash left over because the sum does not divide exactly, but the manager buying £7 units can buy 14.29 units.

Can my PEP buy USM stocks?
Yes. Originally it was proposed that shares quoted on the Stock Exchange's Unlisted Securities Market would not be eligible for PEP benefits. These plans were amended to make them acceptable.

What happens with partly-paid shares' next instalments?
Shares such as British Telecom's, TSB's, Rolls-Royce's and those offered in the BP issue in the autumn of 1987 were offered 'partly-paid' – that is, while they may have been sold at, say 130p, only 50p had to be subscribed immediately, a second instalment would be due some months later, and possibly a third some months after that.

The BP shares offered in October 1987 required £1.20 to be paid then, with another £1.05 due on August 30, 1988, and the final £1.05 to be paid by April 27, 1989. If an investor had been able to buy 2,000 shares at the 1987 price, utilising the full £2,400 PEP allowance, the £2,100 due the following year could be found either from that PEP now selling part of its shares to produce sufficient cash, or a subsequent PEP started for the following year could use its money to pay the second instalment. In the latter case, the shareholding would be split between the two PEPs in proportion to the amount subscribed by each. The £2,100 due in 1989 could come either from a third PEP, or from sales within existing plans holding the BP shares on which the third instalment is due. The PEP manager or investor is, of course, free to sell the shares in the market before the later instalments become due, which sidesteps the problem.

Can I accept rights shares outside my PEP?
Yes. If your PEP owned 1,000 shares in a company which offered you 1,000 more at £1 each and you wanted to take them up but the PEP itself has no cash and you don't want

to sell any of the PEP investments, it is possible for you to use your own non-PEP money.

There could be a tax disadvantage, however. If the new shares are being offered at £1 their market price will be higher, say 130p. The price of the old shares and the newly offered shares would average out at about 115p. Had all the shares been owned outside a PEP the Inland Revenue permits a 'pooling' arrangement for calculating the purchase price when assessing capital gains tax: an investor taking rights shares outside a PEP can effect no pooling arrangement. The shares inside the PEP would fall in price by about 15p – though that cannot be offset against any profits elsewhere for capital gains tax – and the shares bought for £1 outside the PEP would immediately jump in value by about 15p, giving a capital gain which could be taxable when the shares are sold.

Can I accept scrip shares outside my PEP?
No. Shares issued in scrip issues are free, though Chapter 9 explains why their value is limited and the value of the total investment will barely change. They must be put into the plan rather than given directly to the investor.

Who gets the shareholder perks?
A number of companies offer discounts on their goods or services to investors holding a certain number of shares. In theory, PEP investors, because they have a direct ownership of their shares, should be entitled to such perks: in practice, companies are finding it difficult to provide perks because the shares are often held in the PEP managers' names.

Can I invest in 'ethical' investments?
In recent years a number of unit trusts have been launched which buy only ethical investments – shares in companies which do not involve themselves in certain questionable activities or areas, such as alcohol, tobacco, armaments or South Africa. Abbey Life, Buckmaster & Moore, Dominion International, Friends' Provident and N M Schroder

manage such trusts. Of those only Abbey, Dominion and Schroder are plan managers, and only the latter two offer their ethical trusts. Schroder's non-discretionary PEP allows the investor to construct a portfolio including its Conscience fund, while Dominion offers a discretionary PEP comprising its own Fellowship fund and about five shares chosen by stockbrokers Buckmaster & Moore. New Life Financial Services also offers an ethical PEP buying non-contentious shares or buying units in other managers' ethical funds. Although some PEPs specifically choose not to invest in units and some invest only in unit trusts in groups associated with the managers or in specific trusts, many PEPs are free to buy the units of any trusts they choose, including units in ethical trusts. Alternatively, an investor with a non-discretionary PEP could select his own portfolio of morally acceptable shares and/or units.

Must the shares in all my PEPs be the same?
No. Although a discretionary PEP manager may choose to put the same shares at the same time into two existing PEPs started in different years, more usually a person's different PEPs will have different shares. A manager will usually put different shares into a PEP started in January compared with a PEP started by another investor in February and will still leave the original January shares in the first PEP because it is not worth the cost of selling them and buying the February PEP's shares – even though the latter investments may be thought better. It is not worth co-ordinating portfolios in different PEPs therefore, though mature PEPs can be merged into a single large plan.

Some PEP plans are not in your survey
Some PEPs are offered by one company but managed by another. The Abbey National Building Society, for instance, has a PEP, which is actually managed by unit trust group Fidelity International. Some stockbrokers, including Charles Stanley and Spencer Thornton, have PEPs managed by Fidelity, too. A building society can run its own PEP, and the Bradford & Bingley does, which is why it is included in our survey. Building societies must meet the

same standards as other plan managers, but there is also a rule that societies with less than £100m of assets cannot be managers – they can only market other managers' plans. The Abbey National is much bigger than that, but chooses to leave the management to Fidelity. Its charges are identical to Fidelity's own PEP, as are the others managed by that group.

Can I swap from a discretionary to a non-discretionary plan, or vice versa?
It is possible to transfer a PEP, so a PEP holder could take the investments compiled for him or her in a discretionary plan and put them into a non-discretionary plan which the investor then manages. There may be a charge for transferring, however. Switching the other way is more difficult because a discretionary manager is unlikely to want the particular portfolio being offered.

Can I use PEPs as part of a school fees plan?
People devise various methods of investing now to provide school fees which will be payable in future years. In some ways PEPs lend themselves to this because the investment must stay inside the PEP for at least a minimum period. The disadvantage to doing this is that it is impossible to guess the value of the plan at any future date – merely to say that it will be higher than had the same investments been held outside a PEP. The investor could easily find that the proceeds of terminating a PEP were insufficient to meet the school fees and that extra funds had to be found from elsewhere.

Can I borrow against the security of my PEP?
Yes. The beneficial ownership of the investments in the plan must not change – or the tax advantages will be lost if they do. Lenders will give only a proportion of the PEP's value and they may force borrowers to end the PEP prematurely with the loss of the tax advantages, if the investor defaults on the loan.

What if the PEP manager breaks the rules?

The PEP can be transferred to another manager or it can be closed. If it is closed before the end of the qualifying tax year, the investor would be subject to income tax on all dividends received to date and subject to capital gains tax on all profits to date. Arrangements must be made to allow those wanting to continue to transfer to another PEP manager with no loss of the tax advantages. Any particular PEP manager could decline to accept such transfers, however.

What if an investment trust loses its authorisation?

Investment trusts are authorised by the Inland Revenue, but voluntarily or otherwise, some lose that status and become ordinary companies. Normally the trust would still be a permissible investment for a PEP to own, so the investor could accept the change in status; however, when those shares were sold the proceeds could not then be reinvested into another investment trust or unit trust. Sometimes a trust would give warning that it was losing its investment trust status and PEP investors could sell in advance.

Are management charges controlled?

No. The government has deliberately decided to allow managers to set their own charges. These have to be spelt out, but as Chapter 8 describes, they can be high.

Are charges in arrears better than charges in advance?

While it is better to pay a charge later rather than sooner, most PEP managers' annual charges are calculated as a percentage of the shares' value. The advantage of paying annually in arrears rather than in advance is equivalent to the interest which could have been earned on that sum over a year: the disadvantage is that if the value of the share portfolio has risen, the payment in arrears will be a percentage of a higher sum. In a strongly rising market it is better to pay in advance: in weak markets better to pay in arrears – but if the investor thought markets would be weak, he wouldn't be wise to invest at all.

If the stockmarket is crashing as it did in autumn 1987, wouldn't I be better off in cash than shares?

Yes, but there are strict limits on how much can be in cash and for how long. It is possible to buy into shares which do not lose their value because there is a cash bid, however. Hill Samuel had received an 810p a share bid from TSB before the 1987 crash, for instance: even though the market fall reduced TSB's share price and halved the value of most merchant bank shares, Hill Samuel's price stayed up because TSB's offer of 810p cash was still available. A PEP investor needing to be in shares but wanting to avoid the crash could have bought Hill Samuel's shares and waited for TSB to provide the money. Subsequently that cash could be held in the PEP for as long as is permitted, then used to buy different shares at the post-crash prices.

APPENDIX: A PEPS REVIEW

Review of Discretionary PEPs

Abbey Life Investment Services
80 Holdenhurst Road
Bournemouth BH8 8AL
0202 292373

PEP Manager: *Abbey Life Unit Trust & Life Assurance Group*

Invests in: *75% in up to 5 shares; 25% Abbey Income & Growth Unit Trust*

Charges:
  initial: *5%+VAT*
  annual: *1.25%+VAT, half-yearly in arrears*
  meetings: *£40+VAT*
  withdrawal before end of qualifying year: *£35+VAT*
  withdrawal after end of qualifying year: *2 a year free, then £10+VAT*
  share dealing: *up to 0.5%*

Investment:
  Min: *£100* monthly; *£1,200* annually
  Max *£200* monthly; *£2,400* annually

Investors' accounts debited: *1st of month*

Statements: *half-yearly*

Adam & Co Investment Management Ltd
22 Charlotte Square
Edinburgh EH2 4DF
031-225 8484

PEP Name: *Adam PEP*

Manager: *Adam & Co Investment Management, private banking group*

Invests in: *shares or unit trusts*

Charges:
  initial: *£30+VAT*
  annual: *£30+VAT, yearly in advance*
  meetings: *£25*
  withdrawal before end of qualifying year: *£30*
  other: *£25 for additional valuations*
  share dealing: *normal commission*

Investment: *£2,400 annually*

Statements: *half-yearly*

130

Bank of Scotland
PO Box 41
101 George Street
Edinburgh EH2 3JH
031-243 8050

PEP Name: *Level 1 PEP*

Manager: *Bank of Scotland*

Invests in: *at least 3 shares plus 25% in unit trust or investment trust*

Charges:
  initial: *none*
  annual: *2%*
  meetings: *£5*
  withdrawal before end of qualifying year: *£20*
  withdrawal after end of qualifying year: *2 a year free, then £10*
  share dealing: *0.25%*

Investment:
  Min: *£40 monthly; £1,000 annually*
  Max: *£200 monthly; £2,400 annually*

Investors' accounts debited: *15th of month*

Statements: *half-yearly*

Comments: *cheap initially, expensive annually*

PEP Name: *Level 2 PEP*

Manager: *Bank of Scotland*

Invests in: *at least 5 shares*

Charges:
  initial: *none*
  annual: *2%, half-yearly in arrears*
  meetings: *£5*
  withdrawal before end of qualifying year: *£20*
  withdrawal after end of qualifying year: *2 a year free, then £10*
  share dealing: *0.25%*

Investment:
  Min: *£150 monthly; £1,800 annually*
  Max: *£200 monthly; £2,400 annually*

Investors' accounts debited: *15th of month*

Statements: *half-yearly*

Comments: *the zero initial charge is offset by the high 2% a year*

PEP Name: *Standard Life PEP*

Manager: *Bank of Scotland*

Invests in: *Standard Life's UK Equity High Income unit trust*

Charges:
  initial: *none*
  annual: *0.75% year in arrears*
  meetings: *£5*
  withdrawal before end of qualifying year: *£20*
  withdrawal after end of qualifying year: *2 a year free then £10*
  unit trust initial: *5%**
  unit trust annual: *1%*

Investment:
  Min: *£20 monthly; £420 annually*
  Max: *£35 monthly; £420 annually*

Investors' accounts debited: *15th of month*

Statements: *half-yearly*

Comments: *Bank of Scotland manages this PEP for Standard Life (which owns 34% of the bank). The monthly £20 is a cheap way in, but because the PEP buys only units, only £420 can be invested. Why pay two annual charges when the units in the PEP never change? *A 2% bonus is given on investment. Income trusts are good for PEP investors paying high income tax*

PEP Name: *Scottish Unit Managers PEP*

Manager: *Bank of Scotland*

Invests in: *Scottish Unit Managers' Income unit trust*

Charges:
  initial: *none*
  annual: *0.75% yearly in arrears*
  meetings: *£5*
  withdrawal before end of qualifying year: *£20*
  withdrawal after end of qualifying year: *2 a year free, then £10*
  unit trust initial: *5%**
  unit trust annual: *0.75%*

Investment:
  Min: *£20 monthly; £420 annually*
  Max: *£35 monthly; £42 annually*

Investors' accounts debited: *15th of month*

Statements: *half-yearly*

Comments: **investors receive a 2% bonus of extra units. Bank of Scotland manages this PEP for the unit trust group. The £20 is a cheap monthly way in, but because it is units only, investors cannot invest more than £420 a year*

Barclays Bank plc
2nd Floor
Iveco Ford House
Watford WD1 1BP
0923 246353

PEP Name: *Barclayshare Income Portfolio*

Manager: *Barclays Bank*

Invests in: *about 50 shares, investment trusts or Barclays Unicorn General Trust*

Charges:
   initial: *up to £1,200, £28.75; over £1,200, £46*
   annual: *£4 per share at year-end*
   meetings: *none*
   withdrawal before end of qualifying year: *£20 per £1,000*
   share dealing: *none*
   unit trust initial: *5%*
   unit trust annual: *0.75%*

Investment:
   Min: *£20 monthly; £500 annually*
   Max: *£200 monthly; £2,400 annually*

Investors' accounts debited: *13th of month*

Statements: *half-yearly*

PEP Name: *Barclayshare Balanced Portfolio*

Manager: *Barclays Bank*

Invests in: *about 50 shares, investment trusts or Barclays Unicorn General Trust*

Charges:
   initial: *up to £1,200, £28.75; over £1,200, £46*
   annual: *£4 per share at year-end*
   meetings: *none*
   withdrawal before end of qualifying year: *£20 per £1,000*
   share dealing: *none*
   unit trust initial: *5%*
   unit trust annual: *0.75%*

Investment:
   Min: *£20 monthly; £500 annually*
   Max: *£200 monthly; £2,400 annually*

Investors' accounts debited: *13th of month*

Statements: *half-yearly*

PEP Name: *Barclayshare Capital Portfolio*

Manager: *Barclays Bank*

Invests in: *about 50 shares, investment trusts or Barclays Unicorn General Trust*

Charges:
   initial: *up to £1,200, £28.75; over £1,200, £46*
   annual: *£4 per share at year-end*
   meetings: *none*
   withdrawal before end of qualifying year: *£20 per £1,000*
   share dealing: *none*
   unit trust initial: *5%*
   unit trust annual: *0.75%*

Investment:
   Min: *£20 monthly; £500 annually*
   Max: *£200 monthly; £2,400 annually*

Investors' accounts debited: *13th of month*

Statements: *half-yearly*

133

Battey Wimpenny & Dawson
Woodsome House
Woodsome Park
Fenay Bridge
Huddersfield HD8 0JG
0486 608066

PEP Manager: *Battey Wimpenny & Dawson, Stockbrokers*

Invests in: *2 shares and any unit trusts*

Charges:
  initial: *1.5%*
  annual: *1.5%, half-yearly in arrears*
  meetings: *nil*
  withdrawal before end of qualifying year: *up to 10%*
  share dealing: *normal rates*
  unit trust initial: *trusts' charges*
  unit trust annual: *trusts' charges*

Investment:
  Min: £420 annually
  Max: £2,400 annually

Statements: *annually*

Bell Lawrie
Erskine House
68/73 Queen Street
Edinburgh EH2 4AE
031-225 2566

PEP Name: *Bell Lawrie Standard PEP*

Manager: *Bell Lawrie Ltd, Stockbrokers*

Invests in: *3 to 5 shares or unit trusts*

Charges:
  initial: *£25*
  annual: *0.75%, half-yearly in arrears*
  share dealing: *1.65%*
  unit trust initial: *trusts' usual charge*
  unit trust annual: *trusts' usual charge*

Investment:
  Min: £100 monthly; £1,000 annually
  Max: £200 monthly; £2,400 annually

Investors' accounts debited: *1st of month*

Statements: *annually and after investment switches*

Comments: *no charges for meetings or withdrawals*

Blankstone Sington & Co
Martins Building
6 Water Street
Liverpool L2 3SP
051-227 1881

PEP Name: *BS PEP*

Manager: *Blankstone Sington & Co, stockbroker*

Invests in: *Any shares or unit trusts*

Charges:
  initial: *2%*
  annual: *1.5%, yearly in arrears*
  meetings: *£25*
  withdrawal before end of qualifying year: *£15*
  withdrawal after end of qualifying year: *2 a year free*
  share dealing: *nil*
  unit trusts: *no addition charges*

Investment:
  Min: *£1,200 annually*
  Max: *£2,400 annually*

Statements: *half-yearly*

Bradford & Bingley Building Society
PO Box 50
Main Street
Bingley
West Yorkshire BD16 2LW
0800 591771 (Freefone)

PEP Name: *Bradford & Bingley PEP*

Manager: *Bradford & Bingley Building Society*

Invests in: *10 Blue Chip shares*

Charges:
  initial: *5%+VAT*
  annual: *0.75%+VAT from 2nd year*
  meetings: *£50*
  share dealing: *none*

Investment:
  Min: *£50 monthly; £600 annually*
  Max: *£200 monthly; £2,400 annually*

Statements: *half-yearly. Free valuations at any time*

Comments: *a high initial charge, but dealings are free*

Brewin Dolphin & Co
5 Giltspur Street
London EC1A 9DE
01-248 4400

PEP Manager: *Brewin Dolphin & Co, Stockbroker; part of Private Capital Group Ltd.*

Invests in: *3 Blue Chip shares and Brewin International Growth & Income Unit Trust*

PERSONAL EQUITY PLANS

Charges:
  initial: *£24+VAT*
  annual: *0.5%+VAT, yearly in arrears*
  meetings: *£15+VAT*
  withdrawal before end of qualifying year: *£28*
  withdrawal after end of qualifying year: *£28*
  share dealing: *1.65%*
  unit trust initial: *4.75% with 1% discount*
  unit trust annual: *0.75%*

Investment:
  Min: *£600* annually
  Max: *£2,400* annually

Statements: *quarterly*

Valuations: *half-yearly*

Broker Financial Services
Woodbury House
Horsell Park
Horsell, Woking
Surrey
04862 30611

PEP Name: *Practical PEP*

Manager: *Broker Financial Services, licensed dealer*

Invests in: *4–6 shares plus unit trusts*

Charges:
  initial: *3%*
  annual: *1%+£15, half-yearly in advance*
  share dealing: *none*
  unit trust initial: *trusts' own charge, minus a discount*
  unit trust annual: *trusts' own charge*

Investment:
  Min: *£35* monthly; *£420* annually
  Max. *£200* monthly; *£2,400* annually

Investors' accounts debited: *1st of month*

Statements: *half-yearly*

Brown Shipley & Co
30–31 Friar Street
Reading RG1 1AH
0734 595511

PEP Name: *Brown Shipley Managed Scheme*

Manager: *Brown Shipley & Co Bank*

Invests in: *3 or 4 shares plus 25% in Brown Shipley Unit Trust*

Charges:
  initial: *£36+VAT*
  annual: *1.25% on equity element only, yearly in arrears*

withdrawal before end of qualifying year: *1.5%*
share dealing: *1%*
unit trust initial: *trusts' usual charge less 1% discount*
unit trust annual: *trusts' usual charge*

Investment:
  Min: *£500* annually
  Max: *£2,400* annually

Cash invested: *last Friday of month*

Statements: *quarterly*

Comments: *PEP is managed by bank's Heseltine Moss stockbroking subsidiary*

James Capel & Co
James Capel House
PO Box 551
6 Bevis Marks
London EC3A 7JQ
01-621 0011

PEP Name: *James Capel Unit Trust PEP*

Manager: *James Capel & Co, stockbroking subsidiary of Hongkong & Shanghai Banking Corporation*

Invests in: *Capel's income unit trust*

Charges:
  initial: *£30+VAT*
  annual: *1.25% from start of qualifying year*
  meetings: *£25+VAT*
  withdrawal before end of qualifying year: *£30+VAT*

Investment: *£420 lump sum*

Statements: *half-yearly*

Comments: *3.5% discount on unit trust purchases. Not one for would-be big investors*

PEP Name: *James Capel PEP*

Manager: *James Capel & Co, stockbroking subsidiary of Hongkong & Shanghai Banking Corporation*

Invests in: *25% each into 3 Blue Chip shares and Capel's income unit trust*

Charges:
  initial: *£30+VAT*
  annual: *1.25% from start of qualifying year*
  meetings: *£25+VAT*
  withdrawal before end of qualifying year: *£30+VAT*
  share dealing: *1.5%+VAT*

Investment:
  Min: *£100 monthly; £1,200 annually*
  Max: *£200 monthly; £2,400 annually*

Statements: *half-yearly*

Comments: *3.5% discount on unit trust purchases*

Capital House Investment Management Ltd
6 New Bridge Street
London EC4V 6JH
01-353 5050

PEP Name: *Capital House PEP 1*

Manager: *Capital House Investment Management, part of Royal Bank of Scotland*

Invests in: *about 5 Blue Chip shares*

Charges:
  initial: *up to £1,200, £23+VAT; over £1,200, £33+VAT*
  annual: *up to £1,200, 1.5%+VAT; over £1,200, 1.25%+VAT*
  meetings: *£25+VAT each*
  withdrawal before or after end of qualifying year: *£25+VAT*
  share dealing: *1.5%*

Investment:
  Min: *£36 monthly; £300 annually*
  Max: *£200 monthly; £2,400 annually*
Investors' accounts debited: *10th of month*

Statements: *yearly, valuations half-yearly*

PEP Name: *Capital House PEP 2*

Manager: *Capital House Investment Management, part of Royal Bank of Scotland*

Invests in: *about 5 smaller growth companies*

Charges:
  initial: *up to £1,200, £23+VAT; over £1,200, £33+VAT*
  annual: *up to £1,200, 1.5%+VAT; over £1,200, 1.25%+VAT*
  meetings: *£25+VAT each*
  withdrawal before or after end of qualifying year: *£25+VAT*
  share dealing: *1.5%*

Investment:
  Min: *£36 monthly; £300 annually*
  Max: *£200 monthly; £2,400 annually*

Investors' accounts debited: *10th of month*

Statements: *yearly, valuations half-yearly*

PEP Name: *Capital House PEP 3*

Manager: *Capital House Investment Management, part of Royal Bank of Scotland*

Invests in: *one of 6 capital unit trusts*

Charges:
  initial: *3%*
  annual: *1%*
  withdrawal before or after end of qualifying year: *£25+VAT*
  unit trust initial: *3% with 2.25% discount*
  unit trust annual: *1%*

Investment:
   Min: *£35 monthly; £420 annually*

Investors' accounts debited: *10th of month*

Statements: *yearly, valuations half-yearly*

Cawood Smithie & Co
22 East Parade
Harrogate
North Yorkshire HG2 5LT
0423 66781

PEP Name: *White Rose PEP*

Manager: *Cawood Smithie & Co, stockbroker*

Invests in: *1–3 shares*

Charges:
   initial: *1%*
   annual: *none*
   withdrawal before end of qualifying year: *£25*
   share dealing: *2% on first £1,000, then 1%. Min £28 on purchases and £20 on sales*

Investment: *£2,400 lump sum*

Statements: *quarterly*

Comments: *mainly intended for existing clients*

CFS Investment Management Ltd
University House
Lower Grosvenor Place
London SW1W 0EX
01-630 5611

PEP Name: *CFS PEP*

Manager: *CFS (Investment Management), investment managers; part of Comprehensive Financial Services plc*

Restrictions: *existing clients only*

Invests in: *one share*

Charges:
   initial: *nil*
   annual: *£25 yearly in advance*
   other: *none*
   share dealing: *1.25%*

Investment: *£2,400 lump sum*

Statements: *quarterly*

Comments: *a single-share PEP for existing investors*

Commercial Union Assurance PEPS Unit
431 Godstone Road
Whyteleafe, Surrey CR3 0YQ
01-287 7500 ext 4666

PEP Name: *Commercial Union PEP*

Manager: *Ashton Tod McLaren, stockbroker subsidiary of Commercial Union*

Invests in: *3 or 4 shares or unit trusts*

Charges:
   initial: *2%*
   annual: *1% yearly in arrears*
   meetings: *double normal fee*
   withdrawal before end of qualifying year: *3% (£20 min)*
   share dealing: *0.5%*
   unit trust initial: *5% less switching discounts*
   unit trust annual: *trusts' usual charges*

Investment:
   Min: *£20 monthly; £420 annually*
   Max: *£200 monthly; £2,400 annually*

Investors' accounts debited: *5th of month*

Statements: *twice-yearly valuations. Contract notes monthly*

Coutts & Co
Stone Street House
143 Cannon Street
London EC4N 5BJ
01-283 8700

PEP Name: *Coutts Managed Plan*

Manager: *Coutts & Co, Bank*

Restrictions: *existing customers only*

Invests in: *up to 6 shares or unit trusts*

Charges:
   initial: *none*
   annual: *£50+VAT for 1st two years, then 1%+VAT, yearly in advance*
   meetings: *£10 per share*
   withdrawal before end of qualifying year: *£25*
   share dealing: *none*
   unit trust initial: *trusts' usual charge*
   unit trust annual: *trusts' usual charge*

Investment:
   Min: *£1,200 annually*
   Max: *£2,400 annually*

Investors' accounts debited: *10th of month*

Statements: *half-yearly*

140

Dartington & Co
9 The Crescent
Plymouth, Devon PL1 3NP
0752 673663

PEP Name: *Dartington & Co PEP*

Manager: *Dartington & Co Group plc, Investment Group*

Restrictions: *existing clients only*

Invests in: *shares and Dartington Total Performance unit trust*

Charges:
  initial: *£30*
  annual: *1%*
  share dealing: *'normal'*
  unit trusts: *none*

Investment:
  Min: *£1,200 annually*
  Max: *£2,400 annually*

Statements: *half-yearly*

Comments: *no double charging on unit trust*

Dominion Investment Management Ltd
120 Church Street
Brighton
East Sussex BN1 1WD
0273 696000

PEP Name: *Dominion Ethical PEP*

Manager: *Dominion Investment Management, investment arm of Dominion International Group plc*

Invests in: *about 5 'ethical' shares plus 25% in Dominion's Fellowship Unit Trust*

Charges:
  initial: *5% (3% rebate on unit trust)*
  annual: *1.25% on share element, half-yearly in arrears*
  meetings: *£40*
  withdrawal before end of qualifying year: *£35*
  withdrawal after end of qualifying year: *£10*
  share dealing: *0.5%*
  unit trust initial: *5% (see above)*
  unit trust annual: *1%*

Investment:
  Min: *£100 monthly; £1,000 annually*
  Max: *£200 monthly; £2,400 annually*

Investors' accounts debited: *1st of month*

Statements: *half-yearly*

Comments: *one for investors with consciences. Swiss-owned stockbroker Buckmaster & Moore invests 75% of money in companies unconnected with arms, gambling, alcohol, tobacco, South Africa, etc; the other 25% goes into unit trust with similar objectives*

141

Duncan & Toplis (Financial Services) Ltd
3 Castlegate
Grantham
Lincolnshire NG31 6SF
0476 591200

PEP Manager: *Duncan & Toplis (Financial Services) Ltd, Chartered Accountants*

Invests in: *any shares*

Charges:
  initial: *2.5%+VAT*
  annual: *1.25%+VAT, yearly in arrears*
  meetings: *none*
  share dealing: *1.65%*

Investment:
  Min: £1,500 annually
  Max: £2,400 annually

Statements: *annually*

Comments: *a PEP for investors wanting to attend meetings without charge*

Equitable Investment Managers
Walton Street
Aylesbury
Bucks HP21 7QD
0296 393100

PEP Name: *Equitable PEP – Lump-Sum Investment*

Manager: *Equitable Investment Managers Ltd, life assurance company*

Invests in: *about 6 shares from list of 21*

Charges:
  initial: *none*
  annual: *2.5% (+VAT) of fund value at end of first 2 years, then 1% a year in arrears*
  meetings: *£10+VAT each*
  share dealing: *0.25%+0.5% stamp duty*

Investment:
  Min: £1,200 annually
  Max: £2,400 annually

Statements: *annually*

PEP Name: *Equitable PEP – Regular Monthly Investment*

Manager: *Equitable Investment Managers Ltd, life assurance company*

Invests in: *about 6 shares from list of 21*

Charges:
  initial: *none*
  annual: *2.5% (+VAT) of fund value at end of first 2 years, then 1% a year in arrears*
  meetings: *£10+VAT each*
  share dealing: *0.25%+0.5% stamp duty*

Investment:
  Min: £100 monthly
  Max: £200 monthly

Investors' accounts debited: *20th of month*

Statements: *annually*

PEP Name: *Equitable PEP Unit Trust Plan*

Manager: *Equitable Investment Managers, life assurance group*

Invests in: *Equitable Pelican Trust*

Charges:
  initial: *trust's usual charge*
  annual: *trust's usual charge*
  meetings: *£10+VAT*

Investment: £35 monthly

Investors' accounts debited: *20th of month*

Statements: *annually*

Fidelity International
River Walk
Tunbridge
Kent
0800 414161 (freefone)

PEP Name: *Fidelity PEP*

Manager: *Fidelity International Ltd, unit trust subsidiary of American-based investment group*

Invests in: *8 shares with 25% in Fidelity's Growth & Income unit trust*

Charges:
  initial: *5%*
  annual: *1.25%, half-yearly in arrears*
  share dealing: *1.5% maximum*
  unit trust: *no double charging*

Investment:
  Min: *£75 monthly; £1,000 annually*
  Max: *£200 monthly; £2,400 annually*

Investors' accounts debited: *10th of month*

Statements: *annually*

Comments: *investors can use the freefone at any time to check how their PEPs are doing. Fidelity also manages PEPs for the Abbey National Building Society plus several stockbrokers and investment advisors on the same terms.*

James Finlay Co Ltd
Finlay House
10–14 West Nile St
Glasgow G1 2PP
041-204 1321

PEP Name: *James Finlay PEP*

Manager: *James Finlay Corporation, licensed deposit-taker*

Invests in: *4–7 shares or unit trusts*

Charges:
  initial: *1.5%*
  annual: *1.5%, half-yearly in arrears*
  meetings: *£15*
  withdrawal before end of qualifying year: *£25*
  withdrawal after end of qualifying year: *£5*
  share dealing: *1.65%*
  unit trust initial: *3.5%*
  unit trust annual: *1.5%*

Investment:
  Min: *£20 monthly; £200 annually*
  Max: *£200 monthly; £2,400 annually*

Investors' accounts debited: *15th of month*

Statements: *half-yearly*

Comments: *a very low minimum investment*

Fleet PEP Club Ltd
92 Fleet Street
London EC47 1DH
01-353 9632

PEP Name: *Framlington PEP*

Manager: *Fleet PEP Club, friendly society*

Invests in: *4–6 shares with 25% in Framlington Capital unit trust*

Charges:
  initial: *£75+VAT (£25+VAT on subsequent PEPs)*
  annual: *0.5% on shares element*
  meetings: *£20+VAT per share*
  share dealing: *'minimal'*
  unit trust initial: *5%*
  unit trust annual: *0.75%*

Investment: *£2,400*

Statements: *half-yearly*

Comments: *the Fleet Friendly Society manages this PEP for Framlington Unit Trust Group whose own PEP can invest only £420 in units*

Framlington Investment Management Ltd
3 London Wall Buildings
London Wall
London EC2M 5NQ
01-628 5181

PEP Name: *Framlington PEP 87*

Manager: *Framlington Investment Management, part of Framlington Group*

Invests in: *about 25 shares*

Charges:
  initial: *5%*
  annual: *1%+VAT*

Investment: *£420 lump sum*

Statements: *each December 31*

Comments: *PEP 87 is a unit trust from this well-known group. There is no double charging and no exit fees, but investors are limited to just £420. For those who can afford more it's a shame to waste the extra tax benefit. See also the Framlington PEP managed by Fleet, below*

Fraser Henderson Ltd
20 Chiswell Street
London EC1Y 4TY
01-628 0241

PEP Manager: *Fraser Henderson, investment management arm of Baltic plc*

Restrictions: *only for existing clients*

Invests in: *1–8 shares or unit trusts*

Charges:
  initial and annual: *included in clients' existing portfolio charge, quarterly in arrears*
  other: *£5+VAT per transaction*
  share dealing: *1.3% (£10 min)*
  unit trust initial: *trusts' usual charge, but 2% discount on Baltic units*
  unit trust annual: *trusts' usual charge*

Investment:
  Min: *£1,000 annually*
  Max: *£2,400 annually*

Statements: *quarterly*

Comments: *used as addition to clients' existing portfolios*

F.S. Investment Managers
190 West George Street
Glasgow G2 2PH
041-322 3132 ext 470

PEP Name: *F.S. Tax Shelter*

Manager: *F.S. Investment Managers, Unit Trust and Assurance Group*

Invests in: *6 shares and F.S. Balanced Growth unit trust*

Charges:
  initial: *£120*
  annual: *0.2% per month*
  meetings: *£120*
  withdrawal before end of qualifying year: *£50*
  withdrawal after end of qualifying year: *£50 but cash free*
  share dealing: *0.2%*
  unit trust initial: *5.5%*
  unit trust annual: *0.75%*

Investment:
   Min: £1,000 annually
   Max: £2,400 annually

Statements: *half-yearly*

Comments: *the initial charge is high – especially for £1,000 investments, but unit trust double charging is reduced by issuing units at 95% of their offer price*

Gartmore Investment Management Ltd
Gartmore House
16–18 Monument Street
London EC3R 8AJ
01-623 1212

PEP Name: *Gartmore PEP*

Manager: *Gartmore Investment Management, unit trust division of British & Commonwealth plc*

Invests in: *up to 4 shares and Gartmore Global unit trust*

Charges:
   initial: *5%+VAT*
   annual: *1.25%+VAT half-yearly in arrears*
   meetings: *£40+VAT for all shares*
   withdrawal before end of qualifying year: *£25+VAT*
   withdrawal after end of qualifying year: *'small charge'*
   share dealing: *stockbrokers' charges*

Investment:
   Min: £100 monthly; £1,000 annually
   Max: £200 monthly; £2,400 annually

Investors' accounts debited: *1st of month*

Statements: *twice-yearly*

Comments: *no double charging on units*

Gerrard Vivien Grey
Ling House
10/13 Dominion Street
London EC2M 2UX
01-638 2888

PEP Manager: *Gerrard Vivien Grey, stockbroking subsidiary of Gerrard & National Holdings*

Invests in: *any 5 of FTSE 100 shares and unit trusts or investment trusts*

Charges:
   initial: *5%+VAT*
   annual: *1.5%+VAT, half-yearly in arrears*
   meetings: *£10+VAT*
   withdrawal before end of qualifying year: *none*
   withdrawal after end of qualifying year: *one free, then £10+VAT*
   other: *proxy votes, £10+VAT*
   share dealings: *0.75%+VAT*
   unit trust initial: *trusts' usual charges*
   unit trust annual: *trusts' usual charges*

Investment:
    Min: *£1,000* annually
    Max: *£2,400* annually

Statements: *twice yearly or on switches*

Comments: *PEP offers discount on any Henderson unit trust because Henderson does the administration*

Harvard Securities plc
95 Southwark Street
London SE1 0HX
01-928 2109

PEP Name: *Pepshare*

Manager: *Harvard Securities plc, licensed dealer in securities*

Invests in: *shares*

Charges:
    initial: *up to £1,200, £28.75; over £1,200, £96*
    annual: *1%, yearly in arrears*
    meetings: *£10*
    other: *£6 administration charge for each deal: maximum £36 pa*

Investment:
    Min: *£40* monthly; *£480* annually
    Max: *£200* monthly; *£2,400* annually

Statements: *quarterly, valuations annually*

Henderson Administration Ltd
3 Finsbury Avenue
London EC2M 2PA
01-638 5757
PEP Names: *Henderson Growth Portfolio/Henderson Income Portfolio*

Manager: *Henderson Administration unit trust group*

Invests in: *up to 5 shares from FTSE 100 and one Henderson unit trust*

Charges:
    initial: *5%+VAT*
    annual: *1.5%+VAT half-yearly in arrears*
    meetings: *£10+VAT*
    withdrawal after end of qualifying year: *one free a year, then £10+VAT*
    other: *£10+VAT for proxies*
    share dealing: *max 0.5%+VAT*
    unit trust initial: *trusts' usual charges, less discount*
    unit trust annual: *0.5 to 1.25%*

Investment:
    Min: *£1,000* annually
    Max: *£2,400* annually

Statements: *quarterly bargain report, half-yearly valuation*

Comment: *investors have a choice of a growth PEP or income PEP – each including one of Henderson's own unit trusts*

Hill Osborne
Royal Insurance Buildings
Silver Street
Lincoln LN2 1DU
0522 513838

PEP Manager: *Hill Osborne, stockbrokers*

Invests in: *any shares or unit trusts*

Charges:
  initial: *2.5%+VAT*
  annual: *1.25%+VAT yearly in arrears*
  share dealings: *1.65% (£20 min)*
  unit trust initial: *trusts' usual charge*
  unit trust annual: *trusts' usual charge*

Investment:
  Min: *£1,500* annually
  Max: *£2,400* annually

Statements: *annually*

Hill Samuel PEPs
Kintore House
74–77 Queen Street
Edinburgh EH2 4NE
031-225 8525

PEP Name: *Hill Samuel Unit Trust Fund*

Manager: *Hill Samuel, part of TSB Group*

Invests in: *Hill Samuel Income Trust*

Charges:
  initial: *5%*
  annual: *1.5%*
  withdrawal before end of qualifying year: *£25*

Investment:
  Min: *£35 monthly; £420 annually*

Investors' accounts debited: *1st of month*

Statements: *half-yearly*

PEP Name: *Hill Samuel British Industry Fund*

Manager: *Hill Samuel, part of TSB Group*

Invests in: *about 5 shares and Hill Samuel unit trusts*

Charges:
  initial: *5%*
  annual: *1.5%, yearly in arrears*
  meetings: *£50*
  withdrawal before end of qualifying year: *£25*
  share dealing: *none*
  unit trust initial: *5%*
  unit trust annual: *1.5%*

149

PERSONAL EQUITY PLANS

Investment:
  Min: *£50 monthly; £500 annually*
  Max: *£200 monthly; £2,400 annually*

Investors' accounts debited: *1st of month*

Statements: *half-yearly*

PEP Name: *Hill Samuel Aggressive Growth Fund*

Manager: *Hill Samuel, part of TSB Group*

Invests in: *about 12 shares*

Charges:
  initial: *5%+VAT*
  annual: *1.5%, yearly in arrears*
  meetings: *£50*
  withdrawal before end of qualifying year: *£25*
  share dealing: *none*

Investment:
  Min: *£500 annually*
  Max: *£2,400 annually*

Statements: *half-yearly*

C Hoare & Co
37 Fleet Street
London EC4P 4DQ
01-353 4522

PEP Name: *C Hoare PEP*

Manager: *C Hoare & Co, Bank*

Restrictions: *existing clients only*

Invests in: *shares*

Charges:
  initial: *£25+£20 per subsequent investment*
  annual: *1% (£25 min) yearly in advance*
  meetings: *at discretion*
  withdrawal before end of qualifying year: *none*
  withdrawal after end of qualifying year: *none*
  other: *none*
  share dealing: *stockbroker's charge+£6 after 1st purchase*

Investment:
  Min: *£100 monthly; £1,200 annually*
  Max: *£200 monthly; £2,400 annually*

Statements: *each December 31*

Comments: *upper-crust banker*

Roger T. Hulme
28 St Johns Hill
Shrewsbury SYL 1JJ
0743 54999

PEP Name: *Independent PEP*

Manager: *Roger T. Hulme, investment managers*

Invests in: *2 or 3 shares or unit trusts*

Charges:
  initial: *£10*
  annual: *1.25% yearly in arrears*
  meetings: *£20*
  withdrawal before end of qualifying year: *£30*
  share dealing: *1.65%*
  unit trust initial: *trusts' usual charges*
  unit trust annual: *trusts' usual charges*

Investment:
  Min: *£100* monthly; *£1,000* annually
  Max: *£200* monthly; *£2,400* annually

Statements: *half-yearly*

Individual Pension Funds Ltd
4 Memorial Road
Walkden
Manchester M28 5AQ
061-790 1816

PEP Name: *Individual PEP*

Manager: *Individual Pension Funds Ltd, insurance brokers*

Invests in: *any shares or unit trusts*

Charges:
  initial: *4%*
  annual: *1.25% yearly in advance*
  share dealing: *stockbrokers' charges (about 0.4%)*
  unit trust initial: *trusts' usual charges, less discounts*
  unit trust annual: *trusts' usual charges*

Investment: *£100* monthly; *£1,000* annually

Statements: *half-yearly*

Jarvis Investment Management Ltd
7 The Drive
Warwick Park
Tunbridge Wells
Kent TN2 5ER
0892 510515

PEP Name: *Jarvis Plan*

Manager: *Jarvis Investment Management, investment managers*

Invests in: *shares or unit trusts*

Charges:
    initial: *1%+VAT*
    annual: *1%+VAT, yearly in arrears*
    meetings: *£15 per share*
    withdrawal before end of qualifying year: *none*
    withdrawal after end of qualifying year: *none*
    share dealing: *'usual', +stamp duty*
    unit trust initial: *as per trust, but Jarvis' 1% waived*
    unit trust annual: *1%+VAT*

Investment:
    Min: *£20 monthly; £200 annually*
    Max: *£200 monthly; £2,400 annually*

Investors' accounts debited: *4th of month*

Statements: *yearly*

Johnson Fry
Princes House
36 Jermyn Street
London SW1Y 6DT
01-439 0924

PEP Name: *The Johnson Fry PEP*

Manager: *Johnson Fry plc, investment advisers and managers*

Invests in: *one speculative share, usually*

Charges:
    initial: *nil*
    annual: *10% of any profit (min £15), yearly in arrears*
    meetings: *£25*
    withdrawal before end of qualifying year: *£35*
    withdrawal after end of qualifying year: *£5*
    share dealing: *1.65%+VAT*

Investment: *£2,400 lump sum*

Statements: *half-yearly*

Comments: *this PEP is designed as a 'high-risk, high-reward' plan for Johnson Fry's existing well-heeled clients – though it is open to anyone. The annual cost is high – but only if it works. An enterprising use of PEPs*

Kitcat & Aitken & Co
The Stock Exchange
London EC2N 1HB
01-588 6280

PEP Name: *Kitcat & Aitken PEP*

Manager: *Kitcat & Aitken & Co, stockbroking subsidiary of Royal Bank of Canada*

Invests in: *4–6 shares or unit trusts*

Charges:
    initial: *£75*
    annual: *1.5%, yearly in advance*

152

meetings: £225 *initial fee instead of £75, plus 5% pa*
share dealing: *1.65%*
unit trust initial: *trusts' usual charges*
unit trust annual: *trusts' usual charges*

Investment:
  Min: *£1,200 annually*
  Max: *£2,400 annually*

Statements: *quarterly*

Comments: *presumably the meeting fee is to stop investors attending. Presumably it works*

Kleinwort Grieveson Investment Management
PO Box 191
10 Fenchurch Street
London EC3M 3LB
01-623 8000

PEP Name: *Kleinwort Grieveson Managed Equity Plan*

Manager: *Kleinwort Grieveson Investment Management Banking Group*

Invests in: *5 or 6 shares and Kleinwort Barrington General Trust*

Charges:
  initial: *£30+VAT*
  annual: *1%+VAT, yearly in arrears*
  meetings: *£40 per PEP per year*
  withdrawal before end of qualifying year: *£20+VAT*
  other: *£20+VAT for transfer or closure*
  share dealing: *0.5%+VAT per sale and purchase*
  unit trust initial: *3.5%*
  unit trust annual: *0.25%*

Investment: *£2,400 lump sum*

Statements: *quarterly*

Comments: *only the maximum £2,400 can be invested and part goes into Kleinwort's own units*

PEP Name: *Kleinwort Grieveson Managed Unit Plan*

Manager: *Kleinwort Grieveson Investment Management Banking Group*

Invests in: *shares and Kleinwort Barrington General Trust*

Charges:
  initial: *none*
  annual: *1%+VAT yearly in arrears*
  meetings: *n/a*
  withdrawal before end of qualifying year: *£20+VAT*
  withdrawal after end of qualifying year: *none*
  other: *£20 for closure or transfer*
  share dealing: *0.5%*
  unit trust initial: *3.5%*
  unit trust annual: *0.75%*

Investment:
  Min: £20 monthly*; £200 annually
  Max: £42 monthly*; £420 annually

Investors' accounts debited: *1st of month*

Statements: *quarterly*

Comments: **monthly investment for 10 months*

Lancaster Asset Management
King William House
13 Queen Street
Bristol BS1 4NT
0225 447560

PEP Name: *The Lancaster PEP Portfolio*

Manager: *Lancaster Asset Management, investment management company*

Invests in: *about 2 shares*

Charges:
  initial: *£50+VAT*
  annual: *1%, half-yearly in arrears*
  meetings: *£50+VAT*
  share dealing: *stockbrokers' charges*

Investment: *£2,400 lump sum*

Statements: *half-yearly*

Julian Lang Financial Services Ltd
St Helens
1 Undershaft
London EC3A 8JR
01-623 1026

PEP Manager: *Julian Lang Financial Services, financial adviser*

Restrictions: *existing clients only*

Invests in: *up to two shares and/or unit trusts*
  initial: *3%*
  annual: *1% yearly advance*
  withdrawal before end of qualifying year: *3%*
  share dealing: *stockbrokers' charges*
  unit trust initial: *3%*

Investment: *£2,400 lump sum*

Statements: *half-yearly*

Comments: *allows free attendance at meetings*

Laurence Keen & Co
Basildon House, Moorgate
London EC2R 6AH
01-600 9100

PEP Name: *Laurence Keen PEP*

Manager: *Laurence Keen & Co, stockbroker*

Invests in: *one share*

Charges:
    initial: *1%*
    annual: *1% yearly in advance*
    meetings: *£15 per share*
    withdrawal before end of qualifying year: £40
    withdrawal after end of qualifying year: £40
    other: *none*
    share dealing: *1.65%*

Investment:
    Min: £1,000 annually
    Max: £2,400 annually

Statements: *half-yearly*

Comments: *choice of 3 PEPs – Growth, Income or Balanced*

C.P. Lemos
8th Floor, Dunster House
17–21 Mark Lane
London EC3R 7AR
01-626 1187/8

PEP Name: *Advantage UK PEP*

Manager: *C.P. Lemos, investment broker*

Invests in: *shares and unit trusts*

Charges:
    initial: *3% (£20 min.)*
    annual: *1% yearly in advance*
    share dealing: *stockbrokers' charges*
    unit trust initial: *trusts' usual charges*
    unit trust annual: *trusts' usual charges*

Investment: £200 monthly; £2,400 annually

Statements: *annually*

Lloyds Bank PEP Centre
Capital House
1–5 Perrymount Road
Haywards Heath
West Sussex RH16 3SP
0444 418939

PEP Name: *Lloyds Bank Managed PEP*

Manager: *Lloyds Bank*

Invests in: *up to 30 shares and any Lloyds unit trust*

Charges:
 initial: *nil*
 annual: *1% yearly in advance*
 meetings: *£5*
 share dealing: *0.2%*
 unit trust initial: *3% discount on usual charge*

Investment:
 Min: *£25 monthly; £300 annually*
 Max: *£200 monthly; £2,400 annually*

Investors' accounts debited: *1st week of month*

Statements: *half-yearly*

Comments: *low-cost, low minimum PEP able to choose from 14 unit trusts plus shares. Branches everywhere*

PEP Name: *Lloyds Bank Managed PEP*

Manager: *Lloyds Bank*

Invests in: *range of 30 shares*

Charges:
 initial: *nil*
 annual: *1% yearly in advance*
 meetings: *£5*
 share dealing: *0.2%*

Investment:
 Min: *£25 monthly; £300 annually*
 Max: *£200 monthly; £2,400 annually*

Investors' accounts debited: *1st week of month*

Statements: *half-yearly*

Comments: *like Lloyds' other PEPs, cheap and convenient with a £300 start*

PEP Name: *Lloyds Bank Choice PEP*

Manager: *Lloyds Bank*

Invests in: *up to 4 shares from range of 30 blue chips*

Charges:
 initial: *nil*
 annual: *1% yearly in advance*
 meetings: *£5*
 share dealing: *0.2% to 1.5%*

Investment:
 Min: *£25 monthly; £300 annually*
 Max: *£200 monthly; £2,400 annually*

Investors' accounts debited: *1st week of month*

Statements: *half-yearly*

Comments: *non-discretionary version available. No withdrawal charges – as with other Lloyds PEPs. Cheaper share dealing on bank's own 'Choice Sheet' shares*

M&G Financial Services Ltd

M&G House
Victoria Road
Chelmsford CM1 1FB
0245 266266

PEP Name: *M&G Unit Trust PEP*

Manager: *M&G Financial Services Ltd*

Invests in: *one M&G unit trust*

Charges:
  initial: *5%*
  annual: *1%*

Investment: £35 monthly; £420 annually

Investors' accounts debited: *3rd Wednesday of month*

Statements: *annually*

Comments: *a major unit trust group with good long term record — but for anyone who can afford more than £420 part of the PEP allowance has to be forfeited*

Midland Bank PEP Unit

Courtwood House
Silver Street Head
Sheffield S1 3RD
0742 529075

PEP Name: *Midland Bank Managed Plan*

Manager: *Midland Bank*

Invests in: *about 5 shares and Midland's Income unit trust*

Charges:
  initial: *none*
  annual: *1% of share content (£15 min), half-yearly in arrears*
  meetings: *£10*
  withdrawal before end of qualifying year: *2.5% of withdrawn*
  share dealing: *0.2%*
  unit trust initial: *5.25%*
  unit trust annual: *none*

Investment:
  Min: £20 monthly; £200 annually
  Max: £200 monthly; £2,400 annually

Investors' accounts debited: *10th of month*

Statements: *quarterly (extra valuations £10)*

Comments: *very low minimum investment, low cost and no annual double charging. Income units good for high-rate taxpayers and people with no capital gains tax problem*

Philip J Milton & Co

4 Taw Vale
Barnstable
Devon EX32 8NJ
0271 4300

PEP Name: *Philip J Milton Non-discretionary PEP*

Manager: *Philip J Milton & Co, investment consultants*

Invests in: *any shares or unit trusts*

Charges:
    initial: *5%*
    annual: *2%, yearly in arrears*
    meetings: *varies*
    withdrawal before end of qualifying year: *varies*
    share dealing: *stockbroker's charges*
    unit trust initial: *trusts' charges, less discounts*
    unit trust annual: *trusts' charges*

Investment:
    Min: *£75 monthly; £420 annually*
    Max: *£200 monthly; £2,400 annually*

Statements: *annually (extra valuations £12)*

Comments: *high charges*

MIM Ltd
74–78 Finsbury Pavement
London EC2A 1JD
01-588 2777

PEP Name: *MIM Britannia Special Situations*

Manager: *MIM, subsidiary of Britannia Arrow Unit Trust Group*

Invests in: *6–8 shares and MIM Special Features unit trust*

Charges:
    initial: *5%+VAT*
    annual: *1.25%+VAT, half-yearly in arrears*
    meetings: *£35 a year*
    share dealing: *0.2%*

Investment:
    Min: *£50 monthly; £1,000 annually*
    Max: *£200 monthly; £2,400 annually*

Investors' accounts debited: *15th of month*

Statements: *twice-yearly*

Comments: *no double-charging on units*

PEP Name: *MIM Britannia Blue Chip*

Manager: *MIM Ltd, subsidiary of Britannia Arrow Unit Trust Group*

Invests in: *6–8 Blue Chip shares and MIM Britannia Income & Growth*

Charges:
    initial: *5%+VAT*
    annual: *1.25%+VAT, half-yearly in arrears*
    share dealing: *0.2%*

Investment:
    Min: *£50 monthly; £1,000 annually*
    Max: *£200 monthly; £2,400 annually*

Investors' accounts debited: *15th of month*

Statements: *twice-yearly*

Comments: *no double-charging on unit trusts*

Alexander Moffat & Co
13a Alva Street
Edinburgh EH2 4PH

PEP Manager: *Alexander Moffat & Co, Solicitors*

Restrictions: *existing clients only*

Invests in: *up to 4 shares*

Charges:
  initial: *£75+VAT*
  annual: *none*
  share dealing: *max 1%*

Investment: *£2,400 lump sum*

Statements: *annually*

Comments: *a cheap PEP after the initial fee, but only for Moffat's clients with £2,400*

NatWest PEP Offices
11 Old Broad Street
London EC2N 1BB
01-826 8233

PEP Name: *Managed PEP*

Manager: *National Westminster Bank*

Invests in: *3 shares*

Charges:
  initial: *none*
  annual: *2%, half-yearly in arrears*
  meetings: £100
  withdrawal before end of qualifying year: £25
  withdrawal after end of qualifying year: £25 *for 1st year*
  share dealing: 0.2%

Investment:
  Min: *£20 monthly; £500 annually*
  Max: *£200 monthly; £2,400 annually*

Investors' accounts debited: *28th of month*

Statements: *monthly with half-yearly valuations*

Comments: *cheap PEP with low investment limits*

Neilson Milnes Ltd
Martins Buildings
4 Water Street
Liverpool L2 3UF
051-236 6666

159

PEP Name: *Vintage Managed UK Special Situations Plan*

Manager: *Neilson Milnes Ltd, stockbroker*

Invests in: *about 10 shares and any unit trusts*

Charges:
  initial: 3%
  annual: 1% *yearly in arrears*
  meetings: £10
  withdrawal before end of qualifying year: £50
  withdrawal after end of qualifying year: 0.5%
  share dealing: 1.5%
  unit trust initial: *trusts' usual charges less discount*
  unit trust annual: 1%

Investment:
  Min: £600 annually
  Max: £2,400 annually

Statements: *half-yearly*

New Life Financial Services Ltd
31 Oxford Street
Southampton
Hants SO1 1DN
0703 334727

PEP Name: *New Life Shelter Plan*

Manager: *New Life Financial Services, investment managers*

Invests in: *ethical shares or unit trusts*

Charges:
  initial: £15
  annual: 0.5% *(min £20) plus 5% of profits, quarterly in arrears*
  meetings: *annual charge rises to 0.75% (min £40)*
  withdrawal before end of qualifying year: 15% *of value*
  share dealing: *stockbrokers' charges*
  unit trust initial: *trusts' usual charges, less discount*
  unit trust annual: *trusts' usual charges*

Investment:
  Min: £25 monthly; £300 annually
  Max: £200 monthly; £2,400 annually

Investors' accounts debited: *5th of month*

Statements: *quarterly*

Comments: *invests only in non-contentious investments, but some charges are not cheap*

NFU Mutual Group
Tiddington Road
Stratford-upon-Avon
Warwickshire CV37 7BJ
0789 204211

PEP name: *NFU Mutual Managed PEP*

Manager: *Kleinwort Grieveson Investment Management Banking Group*

Invests in: *5 or 6 shares and Avon Equity Unit Trust*

Charges:
  initial: *2%+VAT*
  annual: *1% yearly in arrears*
  meetings: *£40 per plan per year*
  withdrawal before end of qualifying year: *£20+VAT*
  other: *£20+VAT for transfer or closure*
  share dealing: *0.5% per sale and purchase*
  unit trust initial: *5.25%*
  unit trust annual: *1%*

Investment: *£2,400 lump sum*

Statements: *quarterly*

Comments: *only the £2,400 PEP maximum can be invested. Kleinwort manages plan for NFU; PEP buys NFU's Avon units*

Northcote & Co
Veritas House
119 Finsbury Pavement
London EC2A 1JJ
01-028 8121 ext 242

PEP Manager: *Northcote & Co, stockbroker*

Invests in: *about 3 shares*

Charges:
  initial: *£40+VAT; £20+VAT for later plans*
  annual: *1% yearly in advance*
  meetings: *£190+VAT+5% pa*
  share dealing: *1.65%+VAT*

Investment
  Min: *£1,000 annually*
  Max: *£2,400 annually*

Statements: *quarterly*

Prudential Holborn PEPs Ltd
Valentines House
51/69 Ilford Hill
Ilford, Essex IG1 2DL
01-478 3377, or Linkline 0800 345345

PEP Name: *Holborn Equiplan*

Manager: *Prudential Holborn PEPs Ltd, part of Prudential Corporation plc*

Invests in: *about 20 shares or Prudential unit trusts*

Charges:
  initial: *none*
  annual: *2% annually in arrears from 2nd year*
  meetings: *10% of sum invested*
  share dealing: *none*
  unit trust initial: *none*
  unit trust annual: *trusts' usual charge*

161

Investment:
  Min: *£600 annually*
  Max: *£2,400 annually*

Statements: *quarterly*

Comments: *cheap share dealing but a very high charge for attending meetings*

PEP Name: *Holborn Uniplan*

Manager: *Prudential Holborn PEPs Ltd, part of Prudential Corporation plc*

Invests in: *any of the Pru's 13 unit trusts*

Charges:
  initial: *unit trusts' usual charges*
  annual: *unit trusts' usual charges*

Investment: *£420 lump sum*

Statements: *quarterly*

Comments: *the Pru's £420 ceiling is limiting to bigger investors*

Quilter Goodison
Garrard House
31–45 Gresham Street
London EC2V 2LH
01-600 4177

PEP Manager: *Quilter Goodison, stockbroking subsidiary of French bank, Paribas*

Invests in: *6–8 shares*

Charges:
  initial: *3%*
  annual: *1%, half-yearly in advance*
  withdrawal before end of qualifying year: *1%*
  share dealing: *none*

Investment: *£2,400*

Rathbone Bros & Co
Port of Liverpool Building
Pier Head
Liverpool L3 7NW
051-236 8674

PEP Name: *Rathbone Bros PEP*

Manager: *Rathbone Bros & Co, investment bank*

Restrictions: *existing clients only*

Invests in: *shares*

Charges:
  initial: *none, but 1% at end of first year*
  annual: *1.5% yearly in arrears*
  meetings: *none*

withdrawal before end of qualifying year: 2.5%
share dealing: *'standard terms'*

Investment: *£2,400 lump sum*

Statements: *half-yearly*

Comments: *accepts only a £2,400 lump sum*

Redmayne Bentley
Merton House
84 Albion Street
Leeds LS1 6AG
0532 436941

PEP Name: *Discretionary Special Situations PEP*

Manager: *Redmayne Bentley, stockbrokers*

Invests in: *about 3 shares and 1 unit trust*

Charges:
 initial: *£30*
 annual: *£15 yearly in arrears*
 meetings: *£10+VAT*
 withdrawal before end of qualifying year: *£20+VAT*
 other: *£5 to take up rights issue*
 share dealing: *1.5%–£15 min*
 unit trust initial: *trusts' usual charges+commission on sales*
 unit trust annual: *trusts' usual charges*

Investment:
 Min: *£1,200 annually*
 Max: *£2,400 annually*

Statements: *quarterly*

Comments: *a more aggressive version of the same managers' other discretionary PEP*

PEP Name: *The Discretionary Blue Chip PEP*

Manager: *Redmayne Bentley, stockbrokers*

Invests in: *about 3 shares and 1 unit trust*

Charges:
 initial: *£30*
 annual: *£15 yearly in arrears*
 meetings: *£10+VAT*
 withdrawal before end of qualifying year: *£20+VAT*
 other: *£5 to take up rights issue*
 share dealing: *1.5%–£15 min*
 unit trust initial: *trusts' usual charges+commission on sales*
 unit trust annual: *trusts' usual charges*

Investment:
 Min: *£1,200 annually*
 Max: *£2,400 annually*

Statements: *quarterly*

163

Reigate Asset Management

Lonsdale House
7–11 High Street
Reigate
Surrey
0737 244869

PEP Name: *Rampep 1*

Manager: *Reigate Asset Management, investment managers*

Invests in: *up to 4 shares*

Charges:
  initial: £20
  annual: £20 from 2nd year, yearly in advance
  meetings: £5
  share dealing: max 1.5%

Investment: £2,400 lump sum

Statements: *annually*

Comments: *a cheap flat charge*

Save & Prosper

Hexagon House
28 Western Road
Romford RM1 3LB
0800 282101

PEP Name: *Save & Prosper Unit Trust PEP*

Manager: *Save & Prosper, unit trust group*

Invests in: *any Save & Prosper unit trusts*

Charges:
  initial: *1.5%*
  annual: *1.25%, half-yearly in arrears*
  withdrawal before end of qualifying year: £25
  withdrawal after end of qualifying year: *one free, then £25*
  unit trust initial: *0.25%*

Investment:
  Min: £20 monthly; £250 annually
  Max: £35 monthly; £420 annually

Statements: *half-yearly*

Comments: *no double-charging apart from the extra 0.25% initial charge. A wide units choice from a major group.*

PEP Name: *Save & Prosper Managed Portfolio*

Manager: *Save & Prosper plc, unit trust and pensions group*

Invests in: *10 shares*

Charges:
  initial: *1.5%*

annual: *1.25%, half-yearly in arrears*
meetings: £25
withdrawal before end of qualifying year: £25
withdrawal after end of qualifying year: *one free, then £25*
share dealing: *0.75%*

Investment:
    Min: £50 monthly; £400 annually
    Max: £200 monthly; £2,400 annually

Statements: *half-yearly*

Schaverien Personal Equity Plan
18½ Sekforde Street
London EC1R 0HN
01-251 1626

PEP Name: *Schaverien PEP*

Manager: *Schaverien & Co, stockbrokers*

Invests in: *2 shares*

Charges:
    initial: *£35+VAT*
    annual: *1% yearly in arrears*
    meetings: *£10 a share*
    withdrawal before or after end of qualifying year: *£35 closing charge*

Investment:
    Min: £1,200 annually
    Max: £2,400 annually

Statements: *at least twice yearly*

N M Schroder Financial Management Ltd
Enterprise House
Isambard Brunel Road
Portsmouth PO1 2AW
0705 827733

PEP Name: *N M Schroder PEP*

Manager: *N M Schroder Financial Management, unit trust managers*

Invests in: *up to 10 shares or unit trusts*

Charges:
    initial: *5%*
    annual: *1.25% half-yearly in arrears*
    other: *2.5% switching charge*

Investment:
    Min: £25 monthly; £300 annually
    Max: £200 monthly; £2,400 annually

Investors' accounts debited: *28th of month*

Statements: *half-yearly*

J. Edward Sellers & Partners
17 Portland Square
Bristol BS2 8SJ
0272 429491

PEP Name: *J. Edward Sellers & Partners PEP*

Manager: *J. Edward Sellers, personal financial planners*

Invests in: *2 or 3 shares. Free to invest in unit trusts*

Charges:
    initial: *2%*
    annual: *1% in advance*
    meetings: *£5*
    withdrawal before end of qualifying year: *£25*
    share dealing: *standard commissions*

Investment:
    Min: *£50 monthly; £500 annually*
    Max: *£200 monthly; £2,400 annually*

Investors' accounts debited: *1st of month*

Statements: *twice yearly*

Albert E Sharp & Co
Edmund House
12 Newhall Street
Birmingham B3 3ER
021-200 2244

PEP Name: *Albert E Sharp PEP*

Manager: *Albert E Sharp & Co, stockbroker*

Invests in: *5 shares initially*

Charges:
    initial: *£30*
    annual: *0.75% on lump sum, 1.5% on monthly investments*
    meetings: *varies*
    withdrawal before end of qualifying year: *£10*
    share dealing: *0.5% on sales and purchases*

Investment:
    Min: *£25 monthly; £1,200 annually*
    Max. *£200 monthly; £2,400 annually*

Investors' accounts debited: *28th of month*

Statements: *half-yearly*

Comments: *monthly investment in £25 multiples*

Shaw & Co
4 London Wall Buildings
Blomfield Street
London EC2M 5NT
01-638 3644

PEP Name: *Shaw & Co Managed PEPs*

Manager: *Shaw & Co, stockbrokers*

Invests in: *8–12 shares*

Charges:
   initial: *£36+VAT*
   annual: *1% half-yearly in arrears*
   meetings: *£10 per share*
   withdrawal before or after end of qualifying year: *£36+VAT*
   share dealing: *0.5%*

Investment: *£2,400 lump sum*

Statements: *half-yearly*

Comments: *unit trusts may be used for foreign markets – discounts will be given but Shaw charges 0.5%*

John Siddall & Son
The Stock Exchange
Norfolk Street
Manchester M2 1DS
061-832 7471

PEP Name: *JSS PEP*

Manager: *John Siddall & Son, Stockbrokers*

Invests in: *up to 3 shares*

Charges:
   initial: *£30+VAT*
   annual: *1% yearly, in advance*
   share dealing: *£5+VAT*

Investment:
   Min: *£100* monthly; *£1,200* annually
   Max: *£200* monthly; *£2,400* annually

Statements: *half-yearly*

Silkbarn Management Ltd
Lancaster House
Mercury Court
Tithebarn Street
Liverpool L2 2QP
051-227 2782

PEP Manager: *Silkbarn Management Ltd, investment management subisidary of York Trust plc*

Restrictions: *for existing clients only*

Invests in: *any shares or unit trusts*

Charges:
   initial: *1%+VAT*
   annual: *1%+VAT yearly in advance*
   meetings: *£25+VAT*

Investment: *£1,200 or £2,400 lump sum*

Statements: *twice-yearly*

Spiers & Jeffrey Ltd
36 Renfield Street
Glasgow G2 1NA
041-248 4311

PEP Name: *The Spiers & Jeffrey PEP*

Manager: *Spiers & Jeffrey Ltd, stockbrokers*

Invests in: *shares*

Charges:
  initial: *£24+VAT*
  annual: *1% yearly*
  meetings: *£10*
  withdrawal before or after end of qualifying year: *at manager's discretion*
  share dealing: *1.65%+VAT*

Investment: *£2,400 lump sum*

Statements: *twice-yearly*

Stirling-Gilmour
24 Gilmour Street
Alexandria
Dunbartonshire G83 0DB
0389 52641

PEP Manager: *Stirling-Gilmour, solicitors*

Invests in: *2 shares*

Charges:
  initial: *2%+VAT*
  annual: *1%+VAT yearly in arrears*
  share dealing: *0.65%+stockbrokers' charges*

Investment: *£2,400 lump sum*

Statements: *annually*

T. I. F. TOD
The Grange
Grange Road
West Kirkby
Wirral
Merseyside L48 4EE
051-625 5346

PEP Manager: *T. I. F. Tod, investment manager*

Invests in: *2 or 3 shares*

Charges:
  initial: *2%+VAT*

annual: *1.5%+VAT yearly in arrears*
withdrawal before end of qualifying year: *2.5%+VAT*
share dealing: *£5–£10*

Investment: *£2,400 lump sum*

Statements: *twice-yearly*

Touche Remnant Financial Management Ltd
Mermaid House
2 Puddle Dock
London EC4V 3AT
01-236 6565

PEP Name: *Touche Remnant PEP*

Manager: *Touche Remnant Financial Management, investment managers*

Invests in: *shares, or TR unit trusts and investment trusts*

Charges:
  initial: *none*
  annual: *£50+VAT in first year, then 2% half-yearly*
  meetings: *£25*
  other: *£15 for lodging proxies or requesting company information*
  share dealing: *£5+0.25%*
  unit trust initial: *trusts' usual charge*
  unit trust annual: *trusts' usual charge*

Investment: *£2,400 lump sum*

Statements: *annually*

Comments: *cheap share dealing*

Tower Fund Managers Ltd
5–11 Mortimer Street
London W1N 7RH
01-580 0617

PEP Name: *Tower PEP*

Manager: *Tower Fund Managers, fund management division of Tower Assurance Advisory Services*

Invests in: *10 'alpha' stocks – the most popular shares*

Charges:
  initial: *1.5%*
  annual: *nil in 1st year, then 0.75%*
  meetings: *£25 each*
  withdrawal before end of qualifying year: *2%*

Investment:
  Min: *£1,000 annually*
  Max: *£2,400 annually*

Statements: *twice-yearly*

Comments: *fairly low cost*

Trumark Financial Services Ltd
8 Angel Hill
Tiverton
Devon EX16 6PE
0884 253850

PEP Manager: *Trumark Financial Services, investment advisers*

Invests in: *one share*

Charges:
  initial: *£75+VAT*
  annual: *£25+VAT plus 1% yearly in arrears*
  meetings: *£20 per company*
  share dealing: *1.65% (£25 min)*

Investment: *£2,400 lump sum*

Statements: *yearly*

TSB England & Wales
Charlton Place
Andover
Hampshire SP10 1RE
0264 56789

PEP Name: *TSB PEP*

Manager: *TSB England & Wales, banking group*

Invests in: *any of shares in FTSE 100 index+TSB unit trusts*

Charges:
  initial: *£15 up to £300, then £25, and £40 over £1,000*
  annual: *during qualifiying year: £10 on original investments up to £300, then £15,
  and £25 over £1,000. Mature PEPs 1% (£20 min)*
  meetings: *£10*
  withdrawal before end of qualifying year: *£30*
  other: *may charge for annual reports*
  share dealing: *none*
  unit trust initial: *none*
  unit trust annual: *trusts' usual charges*

Investment:
  Min: *£20 monthly; £250 annually*
  Max: *£200 monthly; £2,400 annually*

Investors' accounts debited: *1st of month*

Statements: *twice yearly. Extra valuations £10*

Comments: *complex charging structure*

Wico Hastings
Clock House
Dogflud Way
Farnham
Surrey GU9 7UD
0252 733345

PEP Manager: *Wico Hastings, part of stockbrokers WI Carr (UK) Ltd*

Invests in: *up to 2 shares*

Charges:
   initial: *£28.75*
   annual: *1%, half-yearly in arrears*
   share dealing: *1.65%*

Investment: *£200 monthly; £2,400 annually*

Investors' accounts debited: *10th of month*

Statements: *half-yearly*

Anthony Wieler & Co Ltd
19 Widegate Street
London E1 7HP
01-377 1010

PEP Name: *Wieler PEP*

Manager: *Anthony Wieler & Co Ltd, investment managers*

Invests in: *up to 5 shares and limited range of unit trusts*

Charges:
   initial: *5%+VAT*
   annual: *1.5%+VAT half-yearly in advance*
   withdrawal after end of qualifying year: *one free, then £10+VAT*
   share dealing: *0.5%*
   unit trust initial: *trusts' usual charges less discount*
   unit trust annual: *1%*

Investment:
   Min: *£1,000 annually*
   Max: *£2,400 annually*

Statements: *quarterly statement, half-yearly valuation*

Comments: *chooses Henderson unit trusts or Wieler's own growth or income funds, but gives 3% discount on Wieler trusts*

Wilcox Young and Company
4 Trinity Street
Dorchester
Dorset
0305 68979

PEP Name: *Wilcox Young PEP*

Manager: *Wilcox Young & Partners, investment managers*

Invests in: *up to 5 shares or unit trusts*

Charges:
   initial: *5%+VAT*
   annual: *1.75%+VAT half-yearly in arrears*
   meetings: *£25*
   withdrawal after end of qualifying year: *one a year free, then £10+VAT*
   share dealing: *0.5%+VAT and stockbrokers' charges*
   unit trust initial: *0.5%+VAT plus trusts' usual charge, less discount*
   unit trust annual: *trusts' usual charges*

Investment:
  Min: *£1,000 annually*
  Max: *£2,400 annually*

Statements: *half-yearly*

Windsor Investment Management Ltd
Windsor House
83 Kingsway
London WC2B 6SD

PEP Name: *Windsor PEP*

Manager: *Windsor Investment Management, investment managers*

Invests in: *Windsor unit trusts: Convertible & Equity, Income, Growth or Property Shares*

Charges:
  initial: *5%*
  annual: *1%+VAT*
  withdrawal before end of qualifying year: *1%+VAT*

Investment: *£420 lump sum*

Statements: *annually*

Comments: *a units-only scheme, and thus limited to £420*

Yorkshire Bank
20 Merrion Way
Leeds LS2 8NZ
0583 441244

PEP Name: *Bank Managed*

Manager: *Yorkshire Bank*

Invests in: *up to 5 shares from list of 30 and Save & Prosper's High Return unit trust*

Charges:
  initial: *none*
  annual: *1.5%, half-yearly in arrears*
  meetings: *£5*
  withdrawal before end of qualifying year: *0.75%*
  withdrawal after end of qualifying year: *0.75%*
  other: *£5 for 'exceptional administration duties'*
  share dealing: *1%*
  unit trust initial: *trusts' usual charges less 2%*
  unit trust annual: *trusts' usual charges*

Investment:
  Min: *£20 monthly; £200 annually*
  Max: *£200 monthly; £2,400 annually*

Investors' accounts debited: *10th of month*

Statements: *half-yearly*

Comments: *no initial charge*

172

Review of Non-Discretionary PEPs

Abbey Life Investment Services
80 Holdenhurst Road
Bournemouth BH8 8AL
0202 292373

PEP Manager: *Abbey Life unit trust and life assurance group*

Invests in: *up to 2 shares from list of 30 in FTSE 100*

Charges:
    initial: *5%+VAT*
    annual: *1.25%+VAT, half-year in arrears*
    meetings: *£40+VAT*
    withdrawal before end of qualifying year: *£35+VAT*
    withdrawal after end of qualifying year: *2 a year free, then £10+VAT*
    share dealing: *1%*

Investment:
    Min: *£1,200 annually*
    Max: *£2,400 annually*

Statements: *half-yearly*

Broker Financial Services
Woodbury House
Horsell Park, Horsell
Woking
Surrey
04862 30611

PEP Name: *Practical PEP*

Manager: *Broker Financial Services, licensed dealer*

Invests in: *4–8 shares*

Charges:
    initial: *3%*
    annual: *1%+£15, half-yearly in advance*
    share dealing: *stockbrokers' charges*
    unit trust initial: *trusts' usual charges, less discounts*
    unit trust annual: *trusts' usual charges*

Investment:
    Min: *£35 monthly; £420 annually*
    Max: *£200 monthly; £2,400 annually*

Investors' accounts debited: *1st of month*

Statements: *half-yearly*

Brown Shipley PEP Managers Ltd
30–31 Friar Street
Reading RG1 1AH
0734 595511

PEP Name: *Brown Shipley Personal Choice PEP*

Manager: *Brown Shipley & Co, bank*

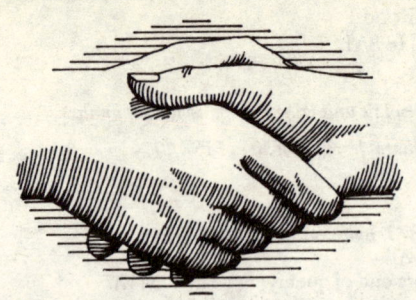

Invests in: *up to 2 shares*

Charges:
   initial: *£36+VAT*
   annual: *0.5% (£15 min) yearly in arrears*
   withdrawal before end of qualifying year: *1.5%*
   share dealings: *1%+VAT on initial purchases, then 1.8%+VAT plus stamp duty*

Investment: *£2,400 lump sum*

Cash invested: *last Friday of month*

Statements: *quarterly*

Comments: *managed by Brown Shipley's Heseltine Moss stockbroking subsidiary*

Capital House Investment Management Ltd
6 New Bridge Street
London EC4V 6JH
01-353 5050

PEP Name: *Capital House PEP 3*

Manager: *Capital House Investment Management, part of Royal Bank of Scotland*

Invests in: *one unit trust from range of 6 capital trusts*

Charges:
   initial: *3%*
   annual: *1%+VAT, half-yearly in arrears*
   withdrawal before or after end of qualifying year: *£25+VAT*
   unit trust initial: *3% with 2.25% discount*
   unit trust annual: *1%*

Investment: *£35* monthly; *£420* annually

Investors' accounts debited: *10th of month*

Statements: *yearly, valuations half-yearly*

PEP Name: *Capital House PEP*

Manager: *Capital House Investment Management, part of Royal Bank of Scotland*

Invests in: *one share*

Charges:
   initial: *£33+VAT*
   annual: *1.25%+VAT, half-yearly in arrears*
   meetings: *£25+VAT each*
   withdrawal before or after end of qualifying year: *£25+VAT*
   share dealing: *1.5%*

Investment: *£2,400 annually*

Statements: *yearly, valuations half-yearly*

Coutts & Co
Stonestreet House
143 Cannon Street
London EC4N 5BJ
01-283 8700

PEP Name: *Coutts Investors Choice*

Manager: *Coutts & Co, bank*

Restrictions: *existing companies only*

Invests in: *any shares or unit trusts*

Charges:
  initial: *none*
  annual: *£50+VAT for 1st two years, then 1%+VAT, yearly in advance*
  meetings: *£10 per share*
  withdrawal before end of qualifying year: *£25*
  share dealing: *1.5% (£20 min)*
  unit trust initial: *trusts' usual charge*
  unit trust annual: *trusts' usual charge*

Investment: *£2,400 lump sum*

Statements: *annually*

Duncan & Toplis (Financial Services) Ltd
3 Castlegate
Grantham
Lincolnshire NG31 6SF
0476 591200

PEP Manager: *Duncan & Toplis (Financial Services) Ltd, chartered accountants*

Invests in: *any shares*

Charges:
  initial: *2.5%+VAT*
  annual: *1.25%+VAT, yearly in arrears*
  meetings: *none*
  share dealing: *1.65%*

Investment:
  Min: *£1,500 annually*
  Max: *£2,400 annually*

Statements: *annually*

Comments: *no charge for meetings*

Eagle Star Trust Company Ltd
1 Threadneedle Street
London EC2R 8BE
01-493 8411

PEP Name: *BAT Industries Equity Plus*

Manager: *Eagle Star, insurance company in BAT group*

Restrictions: *only for existing BAT shareholders*

Invests in: *BAT shares only*

Charges:
  initial: £30
  annual: 1% yearly in arears
  meetings: £75
  withdrawal before end of qualifying year: 1%
  withdrawal after end of qualifying year: 1%
  share dealing: none

Investment:
  Min: £500 annually
  Max: £2,400 annually

Cash invested: 2nd Tuesday each month

Statements: half-yearly

Comments: a PEP to increase BAT investors' existing shareholdings tax-efficiently. That puts a lot of eggs in the same basket though – and why pay £75 to attend a meeting that existing shareholders can attend free? Offset the tax benefits against the usual brokers' costs of buying one share and holding it.

Hill Osborne
Royal Insurance Buildings
Silver Street
Lincoln LN2 1DU
0522 513838

PEP Manager: Hill Osborne, stockbrokers

Invests in: any shares or unit trusts

Charges:
  initial: 2.5%+VAT
  annual: 1.25%+VAT yearly in arrears
  share dealing: 1.65% (£20 min)
  unit trust initial: trusts' usual charge
  unit trust annual: trusts' usual charge

Investment:
  Min: £1,500 annually
  Max: £2,400 annually

Statements: annually

C Hoare & Co
37 Fleet Street
London EC4P 4DQ
01-353 4522

PEP Name: C Hoare PEP

Manager: C Hoare & Co, bank

Restrictions: existing clients only

Invests in: shares

177

PERSONAL EQUITY PLANS

Charges:
    initial: *£25+£20 per subsequent investment*
    annual: *1% (£25 min) yearly in advance*
    meetings: *at discretion*
    withdrawal before end of qualifying year: *none*
    withdrawal after end of qualifying year: *none*
    other: *none*
    share dealing: *stockbroker's charge and £6 after 1st purchase*

Investment:
    Min: *£100* monthly; *£1,200* annually
    Max: *£200* monthly; *£2,400* annually

Statements: *each December 31*

Comments: *upper-crust banker*

Roger T Hulme
28 St Johns Hill
Shrewsbury SYL 1JJ
0343 54999

PEP Name: *Independent PEP*

Manager: *Roger T Hulme, investment managers*

Invests in: *2 or 3 shares or unit trusts*

Charges:
    initial: *£10*
    annual: *1.25% yearly in arrears*
    meetings: *£20*
    withdrawal before end of qualifying year: *£30*
    share dealing: *1.65%*
    unit trust initial: *trusts' usual charges*
    unit trust annual: *trusts' usual charges*

Investment:
    Min: *£100* monthly; *£1,000* annually
    Max: *£200* monthly; *£2,400* annually

Statements: *half-yearly*

Individual Pension Funds Ltd
4 Memorial Road
Walkden
Manchester M28 5AQ
061-790 1816

PEP Name: *Individual PEP*

Managers: *Individual Pension Funds Ltd, insurance brokers*

Invests in: *any shares or unit trusts*

Charges:
    initial: *4%*
    annual: *1.25% yearly in advance*
    share dealing: *stockbrokers' charges (about 0.4%)*

unit trust initial: *trusts' usual charges, less discounts*
unit trust annual: *trusts' usual charges*

Investment: *£100 monthly; £1,000 annually*

Statements: *half-yearly*

Jarvis Investment Management Ltd
1 The Drive
Warwick Park
Tunbridge Wells
Kent TN2 5ER
0892 510515

PEP Name: *Jarvis Plan*

Manager: *Jarvis Investment Management, investment managers*

Invests in: *any shares or unit trusts*

Charges:
   initial: *1%+VAT*
   annual: *1%+VAT yearly in arrears*
   meetings: *£15 per share*
   withdrawal before end of qualifying year: *none*
   withdrawal after end of qualifying year: *none*
   share dealing: *'usual'+stamp duty*
   unit trust initial: *as per trust, but Jarvis' 1% waived*
   unit trust annual: *1%+VAT*

Investment:
   Min: *£20 monthly; £200 annually*
   Max: *£200 monthly; £2,400 annually*

Investors' accounts debited: *4th of month*

Statements: *yearly*

Julian Lang Financial Services Ltd
St Helens
1 Undershaft
London EC3A 8JR
01-623 1026

PEP Manager: *Julian Lang Financial Services, financial adviser*

Restrictions: *existing clients only*

Invests in: *up to two shares and/or unit trusts*

Charges:
   initial: *3%*
   annual: *7% yearly advance*
   withdrawal before end of qualifying year: *3%*
   share dealing: *stockbrokers' charges*
   unit trust initial: *3%*

Investment: *£2,400 lump sum*

Statements: *half-yearly*

Comments: *allows free attendance at meetings*

Lloyd's Bank PEP Centre
Capital House
1–5 Perrymount Road
Haywards Heath
West Sussex RH16 3SP
0644 418939

PEP Name: *Lloyds Bank Choice PEP*

Manager: *Lloyds Bank*

Invests in: *4 shares (from range of 30) or 3 shares plus 1 Lloyds unit trust (from 14)*

Charges:
  initial: *nil*
  annual: *1% yearly in advance*
  meetings: £5
  share dealing: *1.5% for immediate deals (min £20), 0.2% if investors wait**
  unit trust initial: *3% discount off usual charge*
  unit trust annual: *trusts' usual charge*

Investment:
  Min: £25 monthly; £300 annually
  Max: £200 monthly; £2,400 annually

Investors' accounts debited: *1st week of month*

Statements: *half-yearly*

Comments: *Lloyds recommends about 6 companies monthly. *If investors wait for the monthly dealing day charges are cheap*

Midland Bank PEP Unit
Courtwood House
Silver Street Head
Sheffield S1 3RD
0742 529075

PEP Name: *Midland Bank Select Plan*

Manager: *Midland Bank*

Invests in: *up to 4 shares; at least £600 in each*

Charges:
  initial: *none*
  annual: *1% (min £15), half-yearly in arrears*
  meetings: £10
  withdrawal before end of qualifying year: *2.5% of withdrawal*
  share dealing: *1.5% (min £20) plus £5 per transaction*

Investment:
  Min: £600 annually
  Max: £2,400 annually

Statements: *quarterly*

Comments: *the dealing costs are not cheap*

Philip J Milton & Co
4 Taw Vale
Barnstable
Devon EX32 8NJ
0271 4300

PEP Name: *Philip J Milton Non-discretionary PEP*

Manager: *Philip J Milton & Co, investment consultants*

Invests in: *any shares or unit trusts*

Charges:
  initial: 5%
  annual: 2%, *yearly in arrears*
  meetings: *varies*
  withdrawal before end of qualifying year: *varies*
  share dealing: *stockbroker's charges*
  unit trust initial: *trusts' charges, less discounts*
  unit trust annual: *trusts' charges*

Investment:
  Min: £75 monthly; £420 annually
  Max: £200 monthly; £2,400 annually

Statements: *annually (extra valuations £12)*

Comments: *high charges*

MIM Limited
74–78 Finsbury Pavement
London EC2A 1JD
01-588 2777

PEP Name: *MIM Britannia Unit Trust PEPs*

Manager: *MIM, subsidiary of Britannia Arrow Unit Trust Group*

Invests in: *up to 5 unit trusts: European, Income & Growth, Japan, American Growth, Managed Investment Fund*

Charges:
  initial: *trusts' usual charges*
  annual: *trusts' usual charges*

Investment:
  Min: £25 monthly; £300 annually
  Max: £35 monthly; £420 annually

Investors' accounts debited: *15th of month*

Statements: *twice-yearly*

Comments: *units only, so not for people wanting to invest over £420*

NatWest PEP Office
11 Old Broad Street
London EC2N 1BB
01-826 8233

PEP Name: *Shareplan*

Manager: *National Westminster Bank*

Invests in: *any shares*

Charges:
  initial: *£25–£45+VAT, depending on investment*
  annual: *0.75%, half-yearly in arrears*
  meetings: *£100*
  withdrawal before end of qualifying year: *£25*
  share dealing: *£5 per purchase and 1.5% per deal*

Investment:
  Min: *£1,200* annually
  Max: *£2,400* annually

Statements: *monthly reports and half-yearly statements*

Comments: *there are cheaper PEPs at big banks*

Neilson Milnes Ltd
Martins Buildings
4 Water Street
Liverpool L2 3UF
051-236 6666

PEP Name: *Vintage Selected Stocks Plan*

Manager: *Neilson Milnes Ltd, stockbroker*

Invests in: *2 shares from list of 12*

Charges:
  initial: *3%*
  annual: *1% yearly in arrears*
  withdrawal before or after end of qualifying year: *£20 per stock*
  share dealing: *£20*

Investment:
  Min: *£1,200* annually
  Max: *£2,400* annually

Statements: *half-yearly*

NFU Mutual Investment Services
Tiddington Road
Stratford-upon-Avon
Warwickshire CV37 7B
0789 204211

PEP Name: *NFU Mutual Managed PEP*

Manager: *Kleinwort Grieveson Investment Management, merchant banking group*

Invests in: *6 shares and NFU's own Avon Equity unit trust*

Charges:
  initial: *2%+VAT*
  annual: *1%+VAT yearly in arrears*
  meetings: *£40 a year*
  share dealings: *0.5%+VAT*

unit trust initial: *5.25%*
unit trust annual: *1%+VAT*

Investment:
Min: *£120* monthly; *£1,200* annually
Max: *£240* monthly; *£2,400* annually

Investors' accounts debited: *1st of month*

Statements: *half-yearly*

PEP Name: *NFUMIS PEP*

Manager: *NFU Mutual Investment Services, part of National Farmers Union Insurance Society*

Invests in: *group's own Avon Equity unit trust*

Charges:
initial: *5.25%*
annual: *1%+VAT, yearly in arrears*

Investment: *£35* monthly; *£420* annually

Investors' accounts debited: *25th of month*

Statements: *half-yearly*

Comments: *not a PEP for big investors*

Northgate & Co
Ventas House
119 Finsbury Pavement
London EC2A 1JJ
01-628 5121 ext 202

PEP Manager: *Northcote & Co, stockbroker*

Invests in: *shares*

Charges:
initial: *£40+VAT; £20+VAT for later plans*
annual: *1% yearly in advance*
meetings: *£190+VAT+5% pa*
share dealing: *1.65%+VAT*

Investment:
Min: *£1,000* annually
Max: *£2,400* annually

Statements: *quarterly*

P. H. Pope & Son
6 Pall Mall
Hanley
Stoke-on-Trent
0782 202184

PEP Manager: *P. H. Pope & Son, stockbroker*

Invests in: *one or more shares or unit trusts*

Charges:
    annual: *£20 each June 30*
    share dealing: *usual brokers' charge*
    unit trust initial: *trusts' usual charge*
    unit trust annual: *trusts' usual charge*

Investment: *£2,400 lump sum*

Statements: *annual*

Comments: *a nice low-cost PEP for investors wanting to do their own thing – including attending meetings*

Redmayne Bentley
Merton House
84 Albion Street
Leeds LS1 6AG
0532 436941

PEP Name: *The Advisory PEP*

Manager: *Redmayne Bentley, stockbrokers*

Invests in: *any shares or unit trusts*

Charges:
    initial: *£30*
    annual: *£15 yearly in arrears*
    meetings: *£10+VAT*
    withdrawal before end of qualifying year: *£20+VAT*
    other: *£5 to take up rights issue*
    share dealing: *1.5%–£15 min*
    unit trust initial: *trusts' usual charges and commission on sales*
    unit trust annual: *trusts' usual charges*

Investment:
    Min: *£1,200 annually*
    Max: *£2,400 annually*

Statements: *quarterly*

Reigate Asset Management
Lonsdale House
7–11 Hill Street
Reigate
Surrey
0737 244869

PEP Name: *Rampep 2*

Manager: *Reigate Asset Management, investment managers*

Invests in: *up to 4 shares*

Charges:
    initial: *£20*
    annual: *£20 from 2nd year, yearly in arrears*
    meetings: *£5*
    share dealing: *max 1.5%*

Investment: *£2,400 lump sum*

Statements: *annually*

Comments: *a cheap flat charge*

Reyker Securities Ltd
10 Snow Hill
London EC1A 2EB
01-236 7986

PEP Name: *Reyker Securities PEP*

Manager: *Reyker Securities Ltd, financial services company*

Invests in: *any shares or units*

Charges:
   initial: *£100+VAT*
   annual: *1% yearly in advance*
   meetings: *regular, £10+VAT; occasional £5+VAT*
   withdrawal before end of qualifying year: *£25+VAT*
   withdrawal after end of qualifying year: *£25+VAT*
   share dealing: *stockbrokers' charges*
   unit trust initial: *trusts' usual charges*
   unit trust annual: *trusts' usual charges*

Investment: *£2,400 lump sum*

Statements: *twice-yearly*

Comments: *looks expensive*

Save & Prosper
Hexagon House
28 Western Road
Romford RM1 3LB
0800 282101

PEP Name: *Save & Prosper Dealer Plan*

Manager: *Save & Prosper plc, major investment group*

Invests in: *any 'alpha or beta' shares – the most popular stocks*

Charges:
   initial: *1.5%*
   annual: *1.25%, half-yearly in arrears*
   meetings: *£25*
   withdrawal before end of qualifying year: *£25*
   withdrawal after end of qualifying year: *one free, then £25*
   share dealing: *0.75%*

Investment:
   Min: *£400* annually
   Max: *£2,400* annually

Statements: *half-yearly*

A.T. Savings Ltd
Meadow House
64 Reform Street
Dundee DD1 1TJ
0382 201700

PEP Name: *Trust Plan*

Manager: *A.T. Savings Ltd – a part of Alliance Trust investment trust group*

Invests in: *up to 2 shares in 1st year. Only leading companies or Alliance Trust or 2nd Alliance Trust*

Charges:
  initial: *none*
  annual: *none*
  meetings: *£25*
  withdrawal before end of qualifying year: *£5 per investment*
  share dealing: *50p for investment trust purchases and £5 for sales, £5 for other purchases and £15 for sales*

Investment:
  Min: *£25 monthly; £420 annually*
  Max: *£200 monthly; £2,400 annually*

Cash invested: *last 2 weeks of month*

Statements: *on each transaction, and valuations in January*

Comments: *puts investors into one of group's own investment trusts*

Schaverien Personal Equity Plan
18½ Sekforde Street
London EC1R 0HN
01-251 1626

PEP Name: *Schaverien PEP*

Manager: *Schaverien & Co, stockbrokers*

Invests in: *2 shares*

Charges:
  initial: *£35+VAT*
  annual: *1% yearly in arrears*
  meetings: *£10 a share*
  withdrawal before or after end of qualifying year: *£35 closing charge*

Investment:
  Min: *£1,200 annually*
  Max: *£2,400 annually*

Statements: *at least twice yearly*

NM Schroder Financial Management Ltd
Enterprise House
Isambard Brunel Road
Portsmouth PO1 2AW
0705 827733

PEP Name: *NM Schroder PEP*

Manager: *NM Schroder Financial Management, unit trust managers*

Invests in: *one share*

Charges:
  initial: *5%*
  annual: *1.25%, half-yearly in arrears*
  meetings: *£25*
  other: *2.5% switching charge*

Investment:
  Min: *£25* monthly; *£300* annually
  Max: *£200* monthly; *£2,400* annually

Investors' accounts debited: *28th of month*

Statements: *half-yearly*

Shaw & Co
4 London Wall Buildings
Blomfield Street
London
EC2M 5NT
01-638 3644

PEP Name: *Shaw & Co Individual PEP*

Manager: *Shaw & Co, stockbroker*

Restrictions: *only for clients with accumulated gains tax liabilities*

Invests in: *1 share initially*

Charges:
  initial: *£36+VAT*
  annual: *1% half-yearly in arrears*
  meetings: *£5 per share*
  withdrawal before or after end of qualifying year: *£36*
  share dealing: *1.65% (£25 min)*

Investment: *£2,400 lump sum*

Statements: *annually*

John Siddall & Son
The Stock Exchange
Norfolk Street
Manchester M2 1DS
061-832 7471

PEP Name: *JSS PEP*

Manager: *John Siddall & Sons, stockbrokers*

Invests in: *up to 3 shares*

Charges:
  initial: *£30+VAT*
  annual: *1% yearly, in advance*
  share dealing: *1.65%+VAT (£10 min)*

187

PERSONAL EQUITY PLANS

Investment:
   Min: £100 monthly; £1,200 annually
   Max: £200 monthly; £2,400 annually

Statements: *half-yearly*

Wico Hastings
Clock House
Dogflud Way
Farnham
Surrey GU9 7UD
0252 733345

PEP Manager: *Wico Hastings, part of stockbrokers WI Carr (UK) Ltd*

Invests in: *up to 2 shares*

Charges:
   initial: £28.75
   annual: 1%, *half-yearly in arrears*
   share dealings: 1.65%

Investment: £200 monthly, £2,400 annually

Investors' accounts debited: *10th of month*

Statements: *half-yearly*

Yorkshire Bank PLC
20 Merrion Way
Leeds LS2 8NZ
0583 441244

PEP Name: *Customer Choice*

Manager: *Yorkshire Bank*

Charges:
   initial: *none*
   annual: 1.5%, *half-yearly in arrears*
   meetings: £5
   withdrawal before end of qualifying year: 0.75%
   withdrawal after end of qualifying year: 0.75%
   other: £5 per share not on bank's list of 30
   share dealing: 1%
   unit trust initial: *trusts' usual charges less 2% on Save & Prosper High Return*
   unit trust annual: *trusts' usual charge*

Investment:
   Min: £20 monthly; £200 annually
   Max. £200 monthly; £2,400 annually

Investors' accounts debited: *10th of month*

Statements: *half-yearly*

Comments: *no initial charge*

Index